THE GOSPEL OF GRACE

As Revealed to the Apostle Paul

THE GOSPEL OF GRACE

As Revealed to the Apostle Paul

"For I neither received it of man, neither was I taught it, but by the revelation of Jesus Christ" — GALATIANS 1:12.

"Even the mystery which hath been hid from ages and from generations, but now is made manifest in His saints" — COLOSSIANS 1:26.

by
Oliver B. Greene

The Gospel Hour, Inc., Oliver B. Greene, Director
P. O. Box 2024, Greenville, South Carolina

Introduction

Saul of Tarsus, who became Paul the Apostle, will forever stand as one of the most commanding figures in all history — both sacred and secular. Even today, this giant of the faith lives on — through those whom he influenced in life, through the books of the New Testament which he left to us under the dictation of the Holy Spirit, through his interpretation of the Christian faith, and through the magnificent victories he won for Christ.

What we know of him as a person is gleaned in sparse bits — from history, from mention made of him in the Scriptures, and from his own testimony as given in his various writings.

His parents are not named, but from his background as a Hebrew of the Hebrews, of the seed of Abraham, of the tribe of Benjamin, by religion a Pharisee, we know that his family was undoubtedly one of material means. His education under the great Gamaliel in Jerusalem indicates both wealth and social position. He was conscientiously — and *indelibly* — trained in the religion of the Jews, and throughout his ministry his devotion to his own people did not lessen, even though when they rejected his Christ he turned to the Gentiles to preach the Gospel of Grace.

He was born in the city of Tarsus, a metropolis strategically situated on the borderland between the Greek and Jewish worlds and therefore prominent commercially as well as from a military standpoint. It was made a free city by Mark Antony of Rome, and thus Paul could say, "I am a Roman citizen, *free-born.*"

His education and background enabled him to be at home anywhere. As a Roman citizen, he learned of the Roman empire, he learned to respect and was respected by the Roman officials in the provinces. His knowledge of languages, including Greek, made it easy for him to preach understandably wherever he went.

On the other hand, his absolute knowledge and understanding of Jewish law and the Jewish religion enabled him, as a well trained young rabbi, to speak to the Jews in their own language, comprehensively proclaiming the Gospel of Grace as contrasted with and in opposition to the Law of Moses.

Paul did nothing in half-measure. His persecution of the early Church was carried on with such zeal that he is said to have *wrought havoc* among the Christians! By his own testimony we know that he enthusiastically and in all good conscience arrested and imprisoned all professing Christ-followers upon whom he could lay hold. He stood by and consented to the death of Stephen, and I have often wondered if the vision of that young martyr's face, shining with heavenly glory as he died under the stones of the mob, did not linger in Paul's memory until his dying day.

But when he met the Lord Jesus Christ on the road to Damascus, his zeal turned just as ardently to the preaching of Christ — the Son of God, the Messiah who came, was crucified, buried, and was risen again "according to the Scriptures." From that day forward, he never wavered in his proclamation of the Gospel of Grace.

He endured more suffering and persecution than is recorded relative to any other mortal; but with his face stedfastly set toward Heaven and his affections set on things above, he pressed forward — ever onward and upward — toward the prize of the high calling of God in Christ Jesus.

The date of his death is not recorded, but it is thought to be sometime in the years A.D. 65 to 67. Because Paul was a Roman citizen he was granted death by beheading, rather than by crucifixion or other more torturous means. We have no other details of his execution, but we can be sure that, having lived as he lived, he died the same way — as a good soldier of the cross, a loyal ambassador for Christ, a strong witness for the Saviour.

This mighty man, though thought to have been small of stature and unprepossessing in appearance, blazed a pathfinders trail across the frontiers of Christianity, leaving an imprint that will remain as long as the world stands.

Contents

THE GOSPEL OF GRACE

Chapter I

As Revealed to the Apostle Paul

Most great Bible scholars of years past and gone, as well as most living Bible scholars, agree that Paul was greatest among the apostles. I do not profess to be a Bible scholar, but I do sincerely believe that, apart from Jesus Christ, Paul was the greatest man who ever walked upon this earth. Paul is the Moses of the New Testament.

Among the last words spoken by the Lord Jesus to His disciples before He laid down His life a ransom for all are those recorded in John 16:13:

"Howbeit when He, the Spirit of truth, is come, He will guide you into *ALL truth*: for He shall not speak of Himself; but whatsoever He shall hear, that shall He speak: and He will shew you things to come."

Just preceding this, Jesus had been gradually but consistently teaching His disciples of His coming death. He told them of how "He must go unto Jerusalem, and suffer many things of the elders and chief priests and scribes, and be killed, and be raised again the third day" (Matt. 16:21). But now He makes it plain that the time is short, and that He must soon be leaving them:

"Nevertheless I tell you the truth: It is expedient for you that I go away: for if I go not away, the Comforter will not come unto you; but if I depart, I will send Him unto you" (John 16: 7). During His earthly ministry, Jesus was Himself their Comforter; but when He clearly announced His coming departure from them, He promised them another Comforter who would abide with them forever (John 14:16).

In John 16:12 Jesus said to His disciples, "I have yet many things to say unto you, but ye cannot bear them now." He knew exactly how much truth they could receive, He knew the appointed time when they could receive it. Had He revealed, at the beginning of His ministry, some of the things He later revealed to them, those revelations would have been completely beyond the wildest imagination of the apostles.

In John 16:4 He said to them, ". . . These things I said not unto you at the beginning, because I was with you." While He was with them in person, certain things did not need to be said — and if He HAD spoken these tremendous truths at that time they would not have been able to receive and understand them.

Although there were many things that had to remain unsaid at that particular time, Jesus promised that "ALL truth" would be revealed to them eventually — revealed by "the Spirit of truth who was to come after His departure.

The Lord Jesus Christ did not refer to His own words as being either the *fulness* of revelation or the *extent* of the revelation of the glorious Gospel; but He directs the searcher to seek all truth. Therefore they who would know all truth must search the Scriptures, for the revelation given after the crucifixion and after the Day of Pentecost contains truth that Jesus did not reveal during His sojourn here upon this earth.

ALL truth is not recorded in the Gospels, ALL truth was not revealed by the Lord Jesus during His earthly ministry — but all truth was to be *concerning* Him, and does glorify Him.

It was a divine imperative that Jesus Christ come into the world, live here, suffer, die, be buried, and rise again to make possible *the revelation* of all truth. For instance, the phrase "But Christ, being come . . ." prefixes many important teachings concerning His present high priestly office at the right hand of God the Father. It would be well for you to study Hebrews, chapter 9.

Had Jesus declared these tremendous truths while here upon earth, those who heard Him would not have understood such teaching. But now, since Jesus no longer tabernacles in flesh among men, God the Father has been pleased to make known to us the entirety of ALL truth, and if we would know all truth we must seek it in the Scriptures — the Gospel communicated to the Apostle Paul, revealed to him and to others by the Spirit of truth after the Lord Jesus had been exalted to the right hand of the Majesty on high.

In Ephesians 3:1-12 Paul gives this testimony:

"For this cause I Paul, the prisoner of Jesus Christ for you Gentiles, if ye have heard of the dispensation of the grace of God which is given me to you-ward: *How that by revelation He made known unto me the mystery*; (as I wrote afore in few words, whereby, when ye read, ye may understand my knowledge in the mystery of Christ), *which in other ages was not made known unto the sons of men, as it is now revealed unto His holy apostles and prophets by the Spirit*; that the Gentiles should be fellowheirs, and of the same body, and partakers of His promise in Christ by the Gospel: Whereof I was made a minister according to the gift of the grace of God given unto me by the effectual working of His power. Unto me, who am less than the least of all saints, is this grace given, that I should preach among the Gentiles the unsearchable riches of Christ: And to make all men see what is the fellowship of *the mystery, which from the beginning of the world hath been hid in God,* who created all things by Jesus Christ: to the intent that now unto the principalities and powers in heavenly places *might be known by the Church the manifold wisdom of God,* according to the eternal purpose which He purposed in Christ Jesus our Lord: In whom we have boldness and access with confidence by the faith of Him."

I am not suggesting that any part of the Word of God should be preferred above any other. Paul declares that ALL Scripture is inspired:

"All Scripture is given by inspiration of God, and is profitable for doctrine, for reproof, for correction, for instruction in righteousness: That the man of God may be perfect, throughly furnished unto all good works" (II Tim. 3:16, 17).

I am not suggesting that Scriptures have *degrees of authority,* but I am pointing out that *the truth* has been revealed progressively as it *needed* to be (and *could* be) revealed to men who would understand in the Spirit.

I am not suggesting that *any* words could be greater than those that fell from the lips of the Lord Jesus Christ while He

tabernacled among men, but I am attempting to point out that
we need to seek and search out ALL truth — and all truth can be
found only where the Lord Jesus Himself promised it should be
given.

The only possible way for believers to find "all truth" and understand it is to allow the Holy Spirit to reveal it to them. He
(the Holy Spirit) is in the world to glorify the Lord Jesus: "He
shall glorify me; for He shall receive of mine, and shall shew it
unto you. All things that the Father hath are mine: Therefore
said I, that He shall take of mine, and shall shew it unto you"
(John 16:14, 15).

Anyone speaking words of commendation and exaltation concerning himself and his own achievement is not speaking in the
Spirit. All who speak in the Spirit will point men to Jesus and
glorify HIM. The Holy Ghost is in the world to glorify Jesus
Christ — not to glorify man.

The second chapter of Acts records the coming of the Holy
Spirit as promised to the disciples by the Lord Jesus Christ.
The twelve disciples, taught by the risen Christ, were instructed
to tarry in Jerusalem until they were endued with power from on
high. They obeyed the command and tarried until the Day of
Pentecost, and when the Holy Ghost came, *they spoke* — and
what was the theme of their preaching? They proclaimed that
"this is that which was spoken *by the prophet Joel*" (Acts. 2:16).

"Whom the heaven must receive until the times of restitu-
tion of all things, *which God hath spoken by the mouth of all His
holy prophets* since the world began" (Acts 3:21).

The preaching of the disciples as recorded in the first chapters
of the book of Acts consisted primarily of declaration that
those things spoken by the Old Testament prophets had been
literally fulfilled. Until Pentecost, their preaching had been con-
fined primarily to those things foreseen by the prophets and
spoken of by the Lord Jesus. We note further that the epistles
penned down by those who were with Jesus during His earthly
ministry — i.e., the epistles of Peter, John, James and Jude —
contain the following message:

"Wherefore I will not be negligent to put you always *in remembrance* of these things, though ye know them, and be es-

tablished in the present truth. Yea, I think it meet, as long as I am in this tabernacle, to stir you up by putting you *in remembrance*" (II Pet. 1:12, 13).

"This second epistle, beloved, I now write unto you; in both which I stir up your pure minds *by way of remembrance*: That ye may be mindful of the words *which were spoken before by the holy prophets,* and of the commandment of us the apostles of the Lord and Saviour" (II Pet. 3:1, 2).

"Ye therefore, beloved, seeing *ye know these things before* . . ." (II Pet. 3:17).

From the inspired pen of John the Beloved we have these words:

"Brethren, I write no new commandment unto you, but *an old commandment which ye had from the beginning.* The old commandment is the Word which ye have heard from the beginning" (I John 2:7).

"I have not written unto you because ye know not the truth, but because *ye know it* . . ." (I John 2:21).

"Let that therefore abide in you *which ye have heard from the beginning*" (I John 2:24).

"And every spirit that confesseth that *Jesus Christ is come in the flesh* is of God" (I John 4:3).

"And now I beseech thee, lady, not as though I wrote a new commandment unto thee, but *that which we had from the beginning,* that we love one another. And this is love, that we walk after His commandments. This is the commandment, That, *as ye have heard from the beginning,* ye should walk in it" (II John 5:6).

Now notice words given to Jude and penned down for our admonition:

"I will therefore put you *in remembrance, though ye once knew this* . . ." (Jude 5).

"But, beloved, *remember ye the words which were spoken before of the apostles of our Lord Jesus Christ* "(Jude 17).

Thank God for the writings of these men who walked with Jesus, although it is evident that the purpose of their epistles is not to unfold further truth or give us further revelation, but rather to establish the believers in the truth *already known by them through the prophets*, and to bring to our *remembrance* the words spoken by the Lord Jesus while He was here on earth.

Peter does not suggest in any way that God has given to him *all truth*, nor that to him (or to any of his fellow disciples) was given any further revelation *having to do* with all truth. Instead, he directs the believer to the epistles of Paul:

"And account that the longsuffering of our Lord is salvation; even as our beloved brother Paul also according to the wisdom given unto him hath written unto you; as also in all his epistles, speaking in them of these things; in which are some things hard to be understood, which they that are unlearned and unstable wrest, as they do also the other Scriptures, unto their own destruction" (II Pet. 3:15, 16). So you see, beloved, God revealed things to the Apostle Paul that were hard to be understood, even by Peter.

In Paul's testimony before Agrippa, he summarizes his ministry *up to that time* in these words:

"Having therefore obtained help of God, I continue unto this day, witnessing both to small and great, *saying none other things than those which the prophets and Moses did say should come*: That Christ should suffer, and that He should be the first that should rise from the dead, and should shew light unto the people, and to the Gentiles" (Acts 26:22, 23).

Paul gave this testimony in court, just before he was taken from Jerusalem to Rome as a prisoner to appear before Caesar, and under those circumstances his words would have been chosen very carefully. Yet he maintained that up to that very day he had preached nothing save that which had been prophesied in the Old Testament Scriptures.

Therefore we know that up to the time of Acts 26 the Apostle Paul had not preached anything that was not recorded in the books of Moses and the prophets. But by that time, he had completed all of his missionary journeys recorded in the book of Acts. It stands to reason, then, that the Gospel he preached (and that which is recorded in the epistles written to the various churches) *had already been declared and was known by those who heard him.*

What did Paul mean when he said to Agrippa that he had

preached "none other things than those which the prophets and Moses did say should come"? It stands to reason that he did not compromise the Gospel — and according to Paul the heart of the Gospel is the death, burial, and resurrection of Christ. His message as given in Acts 26:23 is threefold:

1 — That Christ should suffer, and that He should be the first to rise from the dead.

2— ". . . And should show light unto the people"

3 — ". . . And to the Gentiles."

Paul preached the Gospel, "the power of God unto salvation," to the Jew first, and also to the Gentiles (or to the Greeks). But whether preaching to Jew, Gentile, barbarian, slave or slave-master, he preached the cross — the death, burial, and resurrection of Jesus "according to the Scriptures." This had been the heart of his message up to his testimony before Agrippa.

To the elders in the church at Ephesus Paul said, ". . . I kept back nothing that was profitable unto you, but have shewed you, and have taught you publickly, and from house to house. . . . Wherefore I take you to record this day, that I am pure from the blood of all men. For *I have not shunned to declare unto you all the counsel of God*" (Acts 20:20, 26, 27).

In Romans 15:19 he declared, "Through mighty signs and wonders by the power of the Spirit of God: so that from Jerusalem, and round about unto Illyricum, *I have fully preached the Gospel of Christ.*"

In these summaries, Paul claims to have exercised a complete ministry — but he did not by any means suggest that this was the completion of his earthly testimony, for we discover from the immediate context of each of these summaries that he is *looking forward*, not knowing the things that were yet to come upon him:

"And now, I go bound in the spirit unto Jerusalem, *not knowing the things that shall befall me there*: save the Holy Ghost witnesseth in every city, saying that bonds and afflictions abide in me. But none of these things move me, neither count I my life dear unto myself, so that I might finish my course with joy, and the ministry, which I have received of the Lord Jesus, to testify the Gospel of the grace of God" (Acts 20:22-24).

"But now having no more place in these parts, and having a great desire these many years to come unto you; whensoever I take my journey into Spain, I will come to you: for I trust to see you in my journey, and to be brought on my way thitherward by you, if first I be somewhat filled with your company. But now I go unto Jerusalem to minister unto the saints. For it hath pleased them of Macedonia and Achaia to make a certain contribution for the poor saints which are at Jerusalem. It hath pleased them verily; and their debtors they are. For if the Gentiles have been made partakers of their spiritual things, their duty is also to minister unto them in carnal things. When therefore I have performed this, and have sealed to them this fruit, I will come by you into Spain. And I am sure that, when I come unto you, I shall come in the fulness of the blessing of the Gospel of Christ" (Rom. 15:23-29).

In Paul's testimony before Agrippa, he quotes words spoken to him by the Lord when he was smitten down on the road to Damascus:

"But rise, and stand upon thy feet: for I have appeared unto thee for this purpose, to make thee a minister and a witness both of these things which thou hast seen, and of those things in the which I will appear unto thee" (Acts 26:16).

When Paul finally arrived in Rome, he called the Jews together, "to whom he expounded and testified the kingdom of God, persuading them concerning Jesus, both out of the law of Moses, and out of the prophets, from morning till evening" (Acts 28:23). Notice that Paul's message here, like that which he preached before this, concerned "none other things than those which the prophets and Moses did say should come." He was speaking to his own brethren, the Jews, and pleading with them concerning Jesus, using the prophecies found in the books of Moses and in the prophets.

Following Acts 26 we find little concerning the things Paul taught, and the book closes with the message concerning him as a prisoner. Thus, the things we learn concerning the apostle and God's dealings with him during his imprisonment can be learned only from his prison epistles — Ephesians, Philippians, Colossians, II Timothy, and Philemon. These epistles should be examined carefully, diligently, by the believer in search of "all truth."

As previously stated, Paul's preaching up to this point involved "none other things than those which Moses and the prophets did say should come." But hear him now — the apostle to whom God revealed the mystery that had been hidden from the beginning of the world:

"Unto me, who am less than the least of all saints, is this grace given, that I should preach among the Gentiles the unsearchable riches of Christ; and to make all men see what is the fellowship of the mystery, which from the beginning of the world hath been hid in God, who created all things by Jesus Christ" (Eph. 3: 8, 9).

"Whereof I am made a minister, according to the dispensation of God which is given to me for you, *to fulfil the Word of God; even the mystery which hath been hid from ages and from generations*, but now is made manifest to His saints" (Col. 1:21, 26).

According to these Scriptures, God revealed, through the pen of Paul, that which had been "hid in God" from the beginning of the world, from all ages and all generations. The mystery that God was about to reveal through this Prince of Apostles was not contained in the Old Testament prophecy, nor was it included in Paul's testimony during the time when he preached "none other things than those which the prophets and Moses did say should come." Therefore, the tremendous truth revealed as this "mystery" must of divine necessity be truth in relation to things *not seen by Moses*, things *not contained in the message of the prophets*, and things *not preached in the first days of the ministry of the Apostle Paul*.

The "mystery" contained further light and deeper truth, to be revealed to Paul and penned down in the epistles dictated to him by the Holy Ghost — epistles which would contain "*all truth.*" The words "to fulfill" in Colossians 1:21 in the pure Greek should read "*to complete.*" The same Greek words appear in Colossians 2:10: "And ye are *complete* in Him," and in Colossians 4:12, ". . . That ye may stand perfect and *complete* in all the will of God."

Therefore, Paul was actually saying, "Whereof I am made a minister according to the dispensation of God which is given to me for you, TO COMPLETE the Word of God. . . ." The "mystery" revealed to the Apostle Paul completed the Gospel message — the Word of God to man. The "mystery" is the fulness of "all truth." Since nothing can be added to that which is complete, believers who know their Bible are not seeking for further revelations or added truth. To Paul, God made known ALL truth, and Paul penned down God's message for us.

Jesus promised, concerning the Holy Ghost, "He will guide you into all truth." This promise is fulfilled in the revelation given to the Apostle Paul by the Holy Ghost, making known the "mystery" *to complete the Word of God.* The ministry of the Holy Spirit is to glorify the Lord Jesus Christ. The purpose of the "mystery" has to do with the exaltation of the Lord Jesus Christ, "far above all principality, and power, and might, and dominion, and every name that is named, not only in this world, but also in that which is to come" (Eph. 1:21).

God's desire for all men is that they might be saved — it is not His will that any should perish; but He also desires that *all believers* may come into the knowledge of *all truth.* To the believer God would make known this mystery, "even the mystery which hath been hid from ages and from generations, but now is made manifest to His saints: To whom God would make known what is the riches of the glory of this mystery among the Gentiles: which is Christ in you, the hope of glory" (Col. 1:26, 27).

To the Ephesians Paul wrote, "Praying always with all prayer and supplication in the Spirit . . . and for me, that utterance may be given unto me, that I may open my mouth boldly, *to make known the mystery of the Gospel,* for which I am an ambassador in bonds: that therein I may speak boldly, as I ought to speak" (Eph. 6:18-20).

Chapter II

God's Chosen Vessel

There is no doubt that the Apostle Paul was keenly aware that God had given him a special and a unique message, to be proclaimed by him and penned down for you and me. As we study Paul's epistles it is evident that he was deeply conscious of the wonder of the Gospel, as well as being alert to the fact that he was Divinely appointed to proclaim this glorious message.

The Gospel of the crucified, buried, risen Christ was super-naturally revealed to Paul — first, as he traveled to Damascus to persecute the Christians there (Acts 9:1-6); then, as he waited through three days and nights of total blindness until the Lord sent Ananias to him (Acts 9:8-19); and finally, during the three years he spent in the desert in Arabia (Gal. 1:17, 18). During these three experiences, God revealed to Paul this glorious Gospel, and made known to him "all truth."

Paul assured the believers in Rome that he was "called to be an apostle, separated unto the Gospel of God" (Rom. 1:1).

In Galatians 1:11, 12 he testified that the message was not his own, nor was it the message of man: ". . . I certify you, brethren, that the Gospel which was preached of me *is not after man. For I neither received it of man, neither was I taught it, but by the revelation of Jesus Christ."*

To Timothy, his son in the ministry, he speaks of "the glorious Gospel of the blessed God, *which was committed to my trust"* (I Tim. 1:11).

In I Thessalonians 1:5 he speaks of the Gospel which "came not unto you in word only, but also *in power, and in the Holy Ghost,* in much assurance."

In II Corinthians 4:3 and II Thessalonians 2:14 he refers to the Gospel as *"OUR Gospel."*

In Romans 2:16 he speaks of "the day when God *shall judge the secrets of men by Jesus Christ according to MY Gospel,"* and in II Timothy 2:8 he says, "Remember that Jesus Christ of the seed of David *was raised from the dead according to MY Gospel."*

In I Corinthians 15:1 and in Galatians 2:2 Paul refers to "the Gospel *which I preach."*

In Acts 20:24 he speaks of "the Gospel of *the grace of God.*

In Romans 1:1 he speaks of *"the Gospel of God,"* and in Romans 1:9 he refers to *"the Gospel of His Son."* In Romans 1:16 he speaks of *"the Gospel of Christ."*

Speaking of various *experiences* in the Gospel, Paul mentions "the *fellowship* of the Gospel (Phil. 1:5), "the *defence and confirmation* of the Gospel" (Phil. 1:7), "the *faith* of the Gospel" (Phil. 1:27), "the *truth* of the Gospel" (Col. 1:5), "the *hope* of the Gospel" (Col. 1:23), the *"afflictions"* of the Gospel (I Thess. 1:6), and the *"light"* of the Gospel (II Tim. 1:10). In Philemon 13 he speaks of himself as being *"in the bonds* of the Gospel."

In his epistles, Paul speaks of the Gospel as relating to various classes of people. He mentions those who are *"called* by the Gospel" (II Thess. 2:14), those who are *"begotten* by the Gospel" (I Cor. 4:15), those who are *"stablished* by the Gospel" (Rom. 16:25); and those who *"obey not* the Gospel" (II Thess. 1:8).

Speaking of himself and of his own divinely appointed ministry, Paul testifies, "Woe is unto me, if I *preach not* the Gospel!" (I Cor. 9:16); and finally, he thunders out a solemn warning to any and all who may pervert the Gospel and preach any other message than that which contains "all truth":

"But though we, or an angel from heaven, preach any other gospel unto you than that which we have preached unto you, let him be accursed. As we said before, so say I now again, If any man preach any other gospel unto you than that ye have received, let him be accursed" (Gal. 1:8, 9).

Today as never before in the history of man, the Gospel dictated to the Apostle Paul by the Holy Ghost is discredited by liberals, modernists, and founders of various cults. Today emphasis is placed on the *ethics* of Jesus, upon His *philosophy of life* as spelled out in the four Gospels. The liberals and modernists cry out, "Return to the Sermon on the Mount!" but my dear reader, if you will search the Sermon on the Mount from the first word to the last, you will not discover one drop of blood — and without the shedding of blood there is no remission of sin!

Ministers today spend long hours preparing sermonettes. They talk about the goodness of God, and of the sinless example of Jesus. But it is not the sinless life of the Saviour nor the supernatural miracles He performed that save the sinner — *it is His death, burial, and resurrection.* The Gospels proclaim a wonderful message, but they point us on to the *epistles* for the deeper, fuller unfolding of "ALL TRUTH."

It is extremely interesting to discover that the Lord Jesus Christ clearly stated how the New Testament would come to be written and given to the Church. Of the Gospels He said, ". . . The Comforter, which is the Holy Ghost, whom the Father will send in my name, He shall teach you all things, and bring all things to your remembrance, whatsoever I have said unto you" (John 14:26).

Of the epistles He said, "Howbeit when He, the Spirit of truth, is come, *He will guide you into all truth . . .*" (John 16:13a).

Pointing forward to the glorious book of the Revelation, He said, ". . . He [the Holy Spirit] shall not speak of Himself; but whatsoever He shall hear, that shall He speak: *and He will shew you things to come*" (John 16:13 b). (And on the lonely Isle of Patmos, the Holy Spirit DID show John the Beloved those "things to come.")

To the Apostle Paul the Holy Spirit dictated these solemn words: "STUDY to shew thyself approved unto God, a workman that needeth not to be ashamed, rightly dividing the word of truth" (II Tim. 2:15). And as we study the writings of this remarkable, Divinely-appointed apostle, we will see that his message contains a perfect balance between the doctrinal and the practical, and also a perfect balance between theology and ethics.

To Paul the Holy Spirit revealed the message that sets men free, keeps them free, and presents them faultless before God the Father. As we study the Gospel preached by Paul we will see that he clearly points out the basic fundamental truths of Christianity, as well as other tremendous truths. We will study the principles of daily Christian living, and also how to overcome the world, the flesh, and the devil.

I sincerely pray that this study will create within the hearts of believers a thirst and hunger for an experience that will cause the ordinary Christian to become extraordinary, and that will cause nominal Christians to become spiritual, victorious saints of God. My prayer is that God will honor the message of the pure Gospel of all truth as we study together.

Chapter III

Condemnation

In this age of higher learning and intellectual enlightenment, there is a tendency to minimize the exceeding sinfulness of sin and look upon it, rather, as a *misfortune*. It is popular to camouflage the exceeding deadliness of sin, its vile character and its corrupting, damning influence upon the sinner, by using such high-sounding phrases as, "Sin is a psychological complex . . . a temperamental lapse . . . a shadow." But as we study Paul's epistles, we will find no such camouflage. Paul fearlessly exposes sin, takes off its mask, and presents it naked and deadly. He pictures sin as it IS, without any frills or sugar-coating. And then in clear, understandable terms he presents *God's perfect remedy* for sin.

The Character of Sin

In Romans 1:18 through 3:20 Paul paints the true picture of sin, a terrible picture of the natural man without Christ. According to the inspired Gospel of Paul, sin is *man's open rebellion* against a holy God, his *opposition* to God's commands, his *insurrection against* God the Creator; and he clearly points out that the character of sin is the deliberate breaking of God's divine law. In this passage from Romans, Paul is in perfect agreement with Isaiah 53:6:

"All we like sheep have gone astray; we have turned every one to his own way; and the Lord hath laid on Him the iniquity of us all."

All men are guilty:

In Romans 1:18-32 Paul points out the fact that the *Gentile* is guilty of sin, and stands condemned before God: "For

the wrath of God is revealed from heaven against ALL ungodliness and unrighteousness of men, who hold the truth in unrighteousness" (Rom. 1:18).

Ungodliness is the root that bears the fruit of unrighteousness
— one is the cause, the other is the effect. Ungodly men live
unrighteous lives. A life of unrighteousness is the product of
sin in the heart. Sin is "the transgression of the law," the exclu-
sion of God from the heart and life of the individual. One who is
ungodly has banished God from his life, lives in open rebellion
against God, and automatically lives unrighteously.

The Jew is guilty before God:

If you will carefully study Romans 2:17-29 you will see that
the Jew, knowing the law of God, *is condemned BY the law*.
The Jews were fanatical concerning the law and its practices,
but the very law they knew and pretended to practice *condemned* them.

"Thou that makest thy boast of the law, through *breaking*
the law dishonourest thou God?" (Rom. 2:23). Israel was the
chosen nation, the elect of God, up to their final rejection of the
Gospel of grace. *Then* God turned to the Gentiles and anointed
Paul as *minister* to the Gentiles. Because of their election and
special privilege as God's chosen people, it was usual for the
Jews to boast of their superior position and the fact that they
were the children of the covenant. They majored on their
religious feasts, festivals, and assemblies. But the Apostle Paul
plainly points out to them that because of their inconsistencies
in daily living, their practices of religious rituals were of no
value and their religious ceremonies were meaningless as having
to do with forgiveness of sin and holiness unto the Lord.

Paul makes it clear that his own people, the Jews, were even
much greater sinners than were the Gentiles, because the Gentiles had sinned without the law (the law was not given to
them); but the Jews to whom the law was given had sinned *in
spite of the law*. They boasted much about the law, but in breaking the law they had dishonored God exceedingly. They could
have been teachers and guides to the Gentiles who were
without God, without hope, aliens to the common-wealth of
Israel and strangers to the covenants; but instead of teaching

and guiding, the Jews had caused the Gentiles to blaspheme
God, as Paul points out in Romans 2:19-24. The Jew had
trampled under foot the law that he valued and prized so
highly, and because the Gentile had observed this inconsistency
on the part of the Jew, he blasphemed instead of worshipping
the Lord God Almighty. Thus, the Jew was more guilty before
God than was the Gentile, because he had more light than did
those who were strangers to the covenants.

The whole world is guilty before God:

"Now we know that what things soever the law saith, it
saith to them who are under the law; *that every mouth may
be stopped, and all the world may become guilty before God*"
(Rom. 3:19).

Notice the stages that lead to ungodliness, and finally cause
God to give up men:

First: "Because that, when they knew God, they glorified
Him not AS God, neither were thankful; but became vain in
their imaginations, and their foolish heart was darkened. Professing themselves to be wise, they became fools, and changed
the glory of the incorruptible God into an image made like to
corruptible man, and to birds, and fourfooted beasts, and
creeping things. WHEREFORE, God also gave them up to
uncleanness through the lusts of their own hearts, to dishonour
their own bodies between themselves" (Rom. 1:21-24).

Second: They "changed the truth of God into a lie, and
worshipped and served the creature more than the Creator, who
is blessed for ever, Amen. For this cause God gave them up
unto vile affections. . ." (Rom. 1:25, 26).

Third: "And even as they did not like to retain God in their
knowledge, God gave them over to a reprobate mind, to do those
things which are not convenient . . . who knowing the judgment
of God, that they which commit such things are worthy of
death, not only do the same, but have pleasure in them that
do them " (Rom. 1:28, 32).

Paul clearly points out that these people *knew* God, but they
refused to glorify Him. They changed the truth of God into a
lie. When we tamper with the Word of God we destroy the
truth, and what we say becomes a lie. The Bible says, "Let

God be true, but every man a liar" (Rom. 3:4); but today men are saying, "Let our religionists re-write the Bible," and in so doing, they make God a liar.

These people of whom Paul speaks did not like to retain God in their knowledge. They removed Him from their thinking; they outlawed worship of the one true God. Because of this, God gave them up. First, He gave up the body; second, He gave up the soul (to vile affections); and third, He gave up the mind (because they did not like to retain God in their knowledge).

Beloved, when God gives up an individual — body, soul, and mind — that individual is destined for an eternity in the fires of hell because there is no way for the Spirit to reach him, and no man can come to God unless he be drawn by the convicting power of the Holy Spirit.

Yes, man knew God — but refused to glorify Him, changed God's truth into a lie, and removed God from his thinking. Therefore, we hear these solemn words: ". . . THOU ART IN-EXCUSABLE, O MAN . . . and thinkest thou this, O man, that judgest them which do such things, and doest the same, that thou shalt escape the judgment of God?" (Rom. 2:1, 3).

Sin is not a vague shadow, it is not to be minimized, it cannot be neutral. SIN IS DEFINITE — and when man deliberately crosses God's will, when man assumes himself to be wiser than the God who created him, THAT IS SIN!

Sin is self-will, whether on the part of an individual or a nation. It was that which caused the mob to cry out in Luke 19:14, "We will not have this Man to reign over us," and the mass of mankind today is still proclaiming, "We will not have this Man to reign over us!"

There are but few individuals on earth today who are willing to allow God to dictate their plan of life and their rules for living. Few indeed are willing to pray in the words of Jesus, "not as *I* will, but as *thou* wilt!" The mass of humanity today is self-willed, demonstrating the spirit of the prodigal son of Luke 15, who demanded his inheritance and took his journey into a far-away country, refusing the protection, love, and instruction that his father would so gladly have given.

Man classifies sin as "little, medium, or big." But there is no such things as "a *little* sin" against a holy God. Sin is big, ugly, loathesome, black as the walls of hell. Sin brings condemnation, and Paul says in Romans 3:9, ". . . We have . . . proved both Jews and Gentiles, that they are ALL UNDER SIN." Thus is set forth the divine verdict of the Holy Judge, the Lord God Almighty, and that verdict concerns the whole human race.

Let us notice the words of the Apostle Paul in Romans 3:10-18; "As it is written, There is none righteous, no, not one: There is none that understandeth, there is none that seeketh after God. They are all gone out of the way, they are together become unprofitable; there is none that doeth good, no, not one. Their throat is an open sepulchre; with their tongues they have used deceit; the poison of asps is under their lips: Whose mouth is full of cursing and bitterness: Their feet are swift to shed blood: Destruction and misery are in their ways: And the way of peace have they not known: There is no fear of God before their eyes."

Now compare the passage just quoted with these words from the Psalmist: "The fool hath said in his heart, There is no God. They are corrupt, they have done abominable works, there is none that doeth good. The Lord looked down from heaven upon the children of men, to see if there were any that did understand, and seek God. They are all gone aside, they are all together become filthy: there is none that doeth good, no, not one. Have all the workers of iniquity no knowledge? who eat up my people as they eat bread, and call not upon the Lord. There were they in great fear: for God is in the generation of the righteous. Ye have shamed the counsel of the poor, because the Lord is his refuge. Oh that the salvation of Israel were come out of Zion! when the Lord bringeth back the captivity of His people, Jacob shall rejoice, and Israel shall be glad" (Psalm 14).

Three things are pointed out in both of these passages:

1. Man without God *has a degraded will*: "There is none righteous, no, not one." Man is not willing to live in righteousness until God works a miracle in his stubborn will and MAKES him willing to serve God and allow the Holy Spirit to dictate his practices of daily living.

2. Man without God *has a blinded intelligence*: "There is none that understandeth." It is utterly impossible for the natural man to understand the things of God: ". . . The natural man receiveth not the things of the Spirit of God: for they are foolishness unto him: neither can he know them, because they are spiritually discerned" (I Cor. 2:14). "But if our Gospel be hid, it is hid to them that are lost: In whom the god of this world hath blinded the minds of them which believe not, lest the light of the glorious Gospel of Christ, who is the image of God, should shine unto them" (II Cor. 4:3, 4).

3. Man without God *has deadened emotions*: "There is none that seeketh after God." Emotionally, the unregenerate is dead to spiritual things. The person who has never been born again does not hunger and thirst after righteousness.

Thus we see that the natural man is not willing to follow God and serve Him until God works a miracle in his heart. Paul and the Psalmist agree that "they are ALL gone out of the way, there is NONE righteous."

Not only are all men under sin, all men are under the condemnation of the curse:

"For as many as are of the works of the law are under the curse: for it is written, Cursed is every one that continueth not in all things which are written in the book of the law to do them" (Gal. 3:10).

Here the Holy Spirit is showing us that because man is under the curse, he is in desperate need of salvation. The law was not given to save. God did not give the law to prevent sin or transgression, but to bring men under a more strict accountability and a more plainly expressed curse: . . . *By the law is the knowledge of sin*" (Rom. 3:20).

"*The law was our schoolmaster to bring us unto Christ . . .*" (Gal. 3:24). "Schoolmaster" here refers to the trusted servant whose responsibility was to care for a boy until he reached the age when he was no longer under a tutor or schoolmaster. Thus the schoolmaster's duty was to keep the boy from physical or moral evil, and to train and prepare him for future life and manhood.

In the same way, the law was given to warn against evil, to

place before us God's standards and show us how far we fall short of those standards. The law shows us that we are all condemned, we are all under the curse; and seeing our condition, we feel our need of a Saviour and look to the Lord Jesus Christ who was made a curse for us (Gal. 3:13).

". . . The law was given by Moses, but grace and truth came by Jesus Christ" (John 1:17). I re-emphasize the Bible fact that the law was not given to save. No one but Jesus ever *kept* God's law perfectly. To His disciples Jesus said, "Think not that I am come to destroy the law, or the prophets: I am not come to destroy, but to fulfil" (Matt. 5:17).

The law states the demands and commands of God — and what God demands, it is a divine necessity that God provide. *In Jesus* God provided One who was able to keep every jot and tittle of the law. *In Jesus* WE are lawkeepers in the sight of God — but *out of Christ* no one can stand before God, *righteous and fit for the kingdom of heaven.*

All are under judgment:

Since all are under sin, it stands to reason that all are under the judgment of Almighty God (Rom. 3:19). But the preaching that is popular today among the masses is not that "all have sinned and come short of the glory of God" and are therefore under the curse and must face judgment. The popular message today talks of the loving God, the gracious, tender God, Father of all mankind — not Almighty God, the Holy Judge.

Today men are invited to unite with the church, follow Christ in baptism by one method or another (depending upon the denomination or the cult); they are invited to do the best they can, live a good life, and perform charitable works. But Paul thunders out in plain language that *apart from Christ*, ALL are hopelessly lost and stand guilty and hell-deserving before a holy God! *IN Christ Jesus* we are delivered from condemnation. In HIM we will not be judged as hopeless sinners — we will be received by God the Father as a son.

Man is a trinity — body, soul, and spirit. The Scriptures clearly testify to this. There is no such thing as being "partially good" or "partially bad." Man without God is totally corrupt, entirely depraved; but *in Christ Jesus* man is totally righteous.

Sin touches every part of man:

Sin kills the spirit, darkens the soul, blights the body. It not only brings condemnation before God, but it works within the sinner utterly to corrupt his whole being. Paul makes this very clear in his epistles.

The *spirit* of the unregenerate man is dead, although in the Scriptures death does not signify *termination*: it signifies separation. Physically, Adam lived for 930 years, but spiritually he died the moment he ate the forbidden fruit. When he disobeyed God, fellowship between himself and God was broken. His act of disobedience separated him from God.

The soul of the unregenerate man is darkened, alienated, unclean and greedy. Paul describes this condition in Ephesians 4:18, 19: "Having the understanding darkened, being alienated from the life of God through the ignorance that is in them, because of the blindness of their heart: Who being past feeling have given themselves over unto lasciviousness, to work all uncleanness with greediness."

The *body* of unregenerate man is desecrated, perverted, unholy, profane, unfit to be the temple of God. Sin cripples, curses, blights the body — a body which was created for God, to be indwelt by God. But the body of *natural* man is *unfit* to be the dwelling place of God.

Romans 3:13-18 paints the terrible picture of man as God sees him outside of Christ. These words were given to the Apostle Paul and he penned them down for our instruction. It is plain to see that Paul did not believe or teach that there is a spark of Divinity in every man! Such teaching is of the devil, for until man is born again through the power of the Word and the Holy Spirit, made new by the miracle of God in his heart, there is no divinity about him nor in him. Man without Christ as Saviour is depraved, corrupted in his affections, alienated from God and given over to lasciviousness, uncleanness, and greed. There is "no fear of God before his eyes."

But when the natural man comes to know God in regeneration and becomes a new creation in Christ Jesus, he DOES fear God: "The fear of the Lord is the beginning of knowledge . . ." (Prov. 1:7). "The fear of the Lord is clean . . ." (Psalm 19:9).

In the Garden of Eden God promised a Saviour for the soul (Gen. 3:15) and in the fulness of time Jesus came, as promised (Gal. 4:4, 5), but He made no provision to redeem the body. To Adam God said, ". . . Dust thou art, and unto dust shalt thou return" (Gen. 3:19). Because of Adam's sin, the body which was meant to be the dwelling place of the most high God was declared of no use to God, and was destined to return to dust; but in the first resurrection the saints of God will receive a NEW body like unto the resurrection body of Jesus (I John 3:1-3; I Cor. 15:42-45, 51-53).

Chapter IV

Justification

We have just seen that man is dead in trespasses and sin
(Eph. 2:1), which means to be entirely cut off from God. The
Apostle Paul clearly sets forth man's utter need because of sin
— sin that is dark and terrible. Then, he immediately declares
the *remedy* for sin and turns on the light of the glorious Gospel
of the grace of God:

"BUT GOD who is rich in mercy, for His great love wherewith
He loved us, even when we were dead in sins, hath quickened
us together with Christ, (by grace ye are saved;) and hath
raised us up together and made us sit together in heavenly places
in Christ Jesus: That in the ages to come He might shew the
exceeding riches of His grace in His kindness toward us through
Christ Jesus. For by grace are ye saved through faith; and that
not of yourselves: it is the gift of God: not of works, lest any
man should boast. For we are His workmanship, created in
Christ Jesus unto good works, which God hath before ordained
that we should walk in them" (Eph. 2:4-10).

In spite of man's wretchedness, God's rich mercy provided
God's great love. Let me point out here that God's grace pre-
cedes His love. God's grace brought God's great love down to
man:

"But we see Jesus, who was made a little lower than the angels
for the suffering of death, crowned with glory and honour; that
He *by the grace of God SHOULD TASTE DEATH FOR
EVERY MAN* . . . Forasmuch then as the children are partakers
of flesh and blood, He also Himself likewise took part of the
same; that through death He might destroy him that had the
power of death, that is, the devil; and deliver them who through
fear of death were all their lifetime subject to bondage. For ver-

ily He took not on Him the nature of angels; but He took on Him the seed of Abraham" (Heb. 2:9, 14-16).

God's great mercy, God's unmerited, unearned, undeserved favor — God's grace — allowed Jesus, the Son of God's love, to take flesh, a body like unto our own bodies, and in that body do what the law could not do because of the weakness of the flesh (Rom. 8:1-3). It was God's grace that allowed Jesus to take our place and suffer the death we should have died, bearing in His own body the sin that man knowingly committed against a holy God.

Jesus took our sins and nailed them to His cross (I Pet. 2:24). In II Corinthians 5:21 Paul clearly states, "For He hath made him to be sin for us, who knew no sin; that we might be made the righteousness of God in Him."

God's grace brought God's love down to man, and *because of God's love*, we can be saved. We love HIM *because He first loved US*. God saves us for the sake of the Son of His love, the Lord Jesus Christ:

"And be ye kind one to another, tenderhearted, forgiving one another, even as God *for Christ's sake* hath forgiven you" (Eph. 4:32).

"I write unto you, little children, *because your sins are forgiven you for His name's sake*" (I John 2:12).

God demands holiness, purity, righteousness, perfection — and what God demands, He provides — through His love and by His grace. In spite of the black picture of man's total failure, the sun rises on that dark horizon:

"BUT NOW the righteousness of God without the law is manifested, being witnessed by the law and the prophets; even the righteousness of God which is by faith of Jesus Christ unto all and upon all them that believe: for there is no difference: For all have sinned, and come short of the glory of God; Being justified freely by His grace through the redemption that is in Christ Jesus: Whom God hath set forth to be a propitiation through faith in His blood, to declare His righteousness for the remission of sins that are past, through the forbearance of God; To declare, I say, at this time, HIS RIGHTEOUSNESS: that He (God) might be just, and the Justifier of him (even a hell-deserving sinner) which believeth in Jesus" (Rom 3:21-26).

There is no greater doctrinal truth from Genesis to Revelation than that contained in these six verses. These words are like so many sparkling gems set against black velvet! They verify the fact that the Word of God is verbally inspired, dictated by the Holy Ghost and penned down by holy men. The treasure contained in these verses could never be described in the words of man. It is beyond man's ability to fully comprehend the tremendous truth set forth here, but as we study and examine these verses we are made to rejoice that even though man had *completely failed God,* God provided a way of escape, even when we were yet without strength and wholly unlovely.

Throughout Paul's epistles we read such phrases as "BUT God . . . BUT NOW. . . ." In this portion of the Word, the expression *"but now"* points back to the foregoing argument concerning condemnation of the whole world — Jew, Gentile, "whosoever." ALL are under sin. Every mouth is stopped and the whole world stands guilty before God. There is nothing man can say. God Almighty, Creator of man and of the universe, declares that ALL are under HIS JUDGMENT, *because of man's sin.*

God warned man, ". . . Of the tree of the knowledge of good and evil, thou shalt not eat of it: *for in the day that thou eatest thereof thou shalt surely die"* (Gen. 2:17). ". . . *The soul that sinneth, it shall die"* (Ezek. 18:4). But man deliberately rebelled against God, knowingly disobeyed Him, and therefore God declared that man is *without excuse,* having no ground on which to plead for mercy. Man has no method provided by his own hands to bring about his own salvation. Without God, man stands in the darkness of despair and the silence of helplessness — without excuse, without righteousness, without salvation.

So it is that we see man at the close of Romans 3:20. Then, through the inspired pen of the Apostle Paul, called and ordained of God to pen down the glorious Gospel of God's grace, we see the brighter side of the picture:

"BUT NOW the righteousness of God . . . is manifested . . ." Without the law, but witnessed by the law and the prophets, God provided righteousness which satisfies His heart and His

command — righteousness that is IN CHRIST JESUS, OUR LORD. The righteousness OF GOD, *provided BY GOD*, has been manifested and set forth before a world that stood in silence — hopeless, helpless, condemned, hell-bound — and that righteousness is at the disposal of each and every condemned sinner who will believe on the Lord Jesus Christ and receive His finished work.

Jesus, *who IS the righteousness of God*, fulfilled every jot and every tittle of the law, and fulfilled every prophecy in minute detail as foretold by the prophets.

This righteousness of God is *"by faith of Jesus Christ."* Only in Jesus can we find righteousness that will satisfy a holy God; but praise and glory be to His name, this righteousness is for *"ALL them that believe!"* It is true that *all have sinned*, and come short of the glory of God. It is just as true that the righteousness of God is provided and presented to all.

"Being justified freely by His grace . . ." Here we see that justification is free, justification is by His grace — and justification is made possible *"through the redemption that is in Christ Jesus."* He paid the sin-debt at the tremendous price of His own blood, and in Him we have redemption. He declared the righteousness of God, that God in HIS righteousness might be just, and yet justify the ungodly through faith in the shed blood of Jesus. Had not Jesus died on the cross, all offerings of the Old Testament would have been in vain — not one drop of blood shed in sacrifices would have availed anything.

Please notice that Jesus was set forth and His blood was shed in order that God the Father could declare His righteousness *for the remission of sins that are PAST* — that is, the sins from Adam to Calvary. The blood of sacrifices — lambs, bulls, pigeons, doves — did not and could not *take away sin.* (In connection with this, please study the entire tenth chapter of Hebrews.) But because of these offerings, God withheld His judgment.

". . . Through the forbearance of God." According to the dictionary, *forbearance* means "an extension of time for the payment of a debt." God was patient with those who obeyed His laws and His commands in offerings, sacrifices of blood as specified in the law. The blood of these animals did not take

away sins, but the blood caused God to forbear. The Holy
Spirit clearly points out in the Scriptures that God had no pleasure in the blood offered from Eden to Calvary (Heb. 10:6,
8), but in the blood of Jesus God found perfect satisfaction because the atoning blood of the spotless Lamb settled the sin-
question once and forever.

From Eden to Calvary, God was patient toward all who offered sacrifices of blood as specified in the law; *but now* the
righteousness of God *without the law* is manifested — yea, the
blood of God's only begotten Son, of whom He said, "This is
my beloved Son, in whom I am well pleased."

No one but Jesus ever completely and perfectly satisfied the
holiness of God, and the only way you and I can please God is
IN JESUS. In Him we have justification from sin, condemnation
is removed, and we are sanctified forever through the one offering of His precious blood.

What Is the Meaning of Justification?

Dr. C. I. Scofield defines justification as *"the judicial act of God
whereby He justly declares righteous the one who believes on
Jesus Christ. The justified believer has been in court only to
learn that nothing is laid to his charge."*

The root meaning of the English word "justified" is "to make
righteous, or to vindicate, or to exonerate." To be justified is to be
acquitted. To be justified in the sight of God is for the guilty person to be reckoned or accounted by God to be righteous — upon
the faith of that individual in the finished work, the shed blood,
of the Lamb of God.

To be justfied before God is to stand in His presence as though
you had never committed a sin. It is to be just as just as Jesus is
just. And truly, we are in that position when we are justified in
Christ.

Paul uses three Old Testament characters to explain the meaning of justification:

1. Abraham: "For what saith the Scripture? Abraham believed God, and it was counted unto him for righteousness"
(Rom. 4:3).

2. David: ". . . David also describeth the blessedness of the

man, unto whom God imputeth righteousness without works, saying, Blessed are they whose iniquities are forgiven, and whose sins are covered. Blessed is the man to whom the Lord will not impute sin" (Rom. 4:6-8).

3. Adam: "Therefore as by the offence of one judgment came upon all men to condemnation; even so by the righteousness of one the free gift came upon all men unto justification of life. For as by one man's disobedience many were made sinners, so by the obedience of one shall many be made righteous" (Rom. 5: 18, 19).

Abraham believed God. He did not simply believe that there IS a God — he *BELIEVED GOD*. Abraham did not work, he did not give, he did not go — he simply believed God, he *exercised* his faith in God, and God counted his faith for righteousness.

David describes the blessedness of the man unto whom God *imputed* "righteousness without works." From this we know that David believed and taught that righteousness is not to be attained, earned, or acquired — but IMPUTED.

Through the offence of Adam, judgment came upon *all men* — in Adam all die; but by the righteousness of One (the Lord Jesus Christ) "the free gift" came upon all men *unto justification of life*. Through the *disobedience of Adam*, all men became sinners; by the *obedience of Jesus*, man can become righteous. Please notice that it is not through the obedience of the *individual*, but through *the obedience of Jesus Christ*. His obedience to the will of God made justification possible, and *apart from him* there IS no justification.

Through justification, God changes the position of a sinner — guilty, helpless, hopeless, and hell-bound — from condemnation to perfect acceptance before God, and, through the finished work of Jesus Christ, counts the sinner to be righteous.

Justification is more than pardon. Pardon is *negative*, justification *is positive*. Let me illustrate:

Suppose a person is guilty of murder and is sentenced to the penitentiary for life. We may assume that this person becomes a model prisoner, and after some years in prison the parole board recommends that the governor pardon that individual.

Upon receipt of his pardon, the prisoner walks out of the penitentiary a free man, with full pardon from the governor of his state — but neither the governor nor any other person on earth could ever justify that person for the crime committed! The crime can never be erased from the record.

True, the prisoner is a free man under the governor's pardon, but the record will never be changed on the record books. By comparison, *when the guilty sinner exercises faith in the finished work of the Lord Jesus Christ,* God reckons the sinner righteous, imputes righteousness to him, and justifies him through the sacrifice of the Lord Jesus Christ. Thus the sinner who is justified is acquitted, exonerated, and stands before God just as though he had never sinned. His record is wiped clean. To be acquitted means that the person in question has committed no crime.

The man who is pardoned leaves the penitentiary with a record of crime that demands a pardon in order for him to be set free, but the man who is *acquitted* walks from the courtroom without a stain upon his character. He is acquitted because there is no evidence that he has committed a crime. And dearly beloved, *when God Almighty looks upon us, covered by the blood, resting in the finished work of Jesus, He sees us as though we had never sinned!* He sees us IN JESUS, with righteousness imputed, "accepted in the Beloved." And we therefore stand justified before God — not just forgiven, not just pardoned, but JUSTIFIED!

This is too wonderful for me! *This is the wonder of the marvelous Gospel of the grace of God given to the Apostle Paul.* The believer is IN CHRIST, Christ is IN THE BELIEVER, and thus God reckons our sins to His account and reckons the righteousness of Christ to US. In the act of justification, God marks all of our sins down to the account of Jesus, and marks to our credit all the righteousness of Christ. Therefore we stand before God just as pure, just as holy, and just as righteous, as the Lord Jesus Christ, for God the Father sees us in His Son, and reckons us as righteous as Jesus is righteous.

When we step inside the pearly gates, justified, we will actually *be* then what God *reckons* us NOW. In His sight we are as

pure as the blood of Jesus, and when we reach heaven we will
actually possess that purity of body, soul, and spirit. We will be
LIKE HIM!

In Christ, the believer is *now*, this very moment, covered by
the precious, sinless blood of Jesus, shrouded by the marvelous
grace of God, wrapped in complete and blessed righteousness;
and the law from Mount Sinai can find neither spot nor wrinkle
in him. Paul asks, "Who shall lay anything to the charge of God's
elect? It is God that justifieth" (Rom. 8:33).

There is no one in heaven or in earth who can lay anything to
the charge of the believer — justified in the eyes of God, perfect,
righteous, and holy. We actually *possess NOW* what we will
experience when we are inside the pearly gates. Positionally, we
now sit together in heavenly places in Christ Jesus, we are hid
with Christ in God.

How Are We Justified?

Through the pen of Paul, the Holy Spirit clearly outlines the
"how" of justification:

Romans 3:24: "Being justified freely by His grace through the
redemption that is in Christ Jesus . . ."

Romans 5:9: ". . . Being now justified by His blood, we shall
be saved from wrath through Him."

Romans 5:1: ". . . Being justified by faith, we have peace with
God through our Lord Jesus Christ."

We are justified by *grace*, by *blood*, by *faith* — not three
methods of justification, but rather, *these three agree in one*:
grace, blood, and faith make justification possible.

1. — *"Being justified . . . by His GRACE*: Grace is the com-
munication of Almighty God to meet the need of mortal man
in every way, and all blessings received by man have their origin
in grace. Grace is unearned, undeserved, unmerited favor from
God to man. Grace is more than love — grace is *love in action*,
directed toward those who have no claim upon God's grace.

Grace is loving one who deserves no love. Grace is being at-
tracted to the unattractive. Grace is demonstrating kindness to
an enemy. It is easy to love those who are our friends, who always say and do kind things toward us. To love someone who

has been good to us is *gratitude* — but *grace* loves where no love is returned. It is easy to love someone who is beautiful and attractive, but *grace* loves the unlovely, the unattractive. Grace is Gods free gift, His unmerited favor, to hell-deserving, unlovely sinners, enemies to God.

Grace was in the heart of God in the beginning: "Forasmuch as ye know that ye were not redeemed with corruptible things, as silver and gold, from your vain conversation received by tradition from your fathers; but with the precious blood of Christ, as of a lamb without blemish and without spot: *Who verily was foreordained BEFORE THE FOUNDATION OF THE WORLD*, but was manifest in these last times for you" (I Pet. 1:18-20).

In Hebrews 2:9 we read, "But we see Jesus, who was made a little lower than the angels for the suffering of death, crowned with glory and honour; *that He BY THE GRACE OF GOD should taste death for every man.*"

From these Scriptures we know that grace was not born in the heart of God because of the sufferings of the Lamb of God on the cross. On the contrary, the cross and the sufferings of Jesus were created by the grace of God, for Peter tells us that redemption was settled and predestined before ever God laid the foundation of this earth. Before God created the dust from which He formed Adam, He perfected and provided redemption.

It was God's grace that allowed Jesus to taste death for every man, and the certainty that He *would* taste death for every man was settled before the foundation of the world was laid. It was by God's grace that the cross was allowed.

The death of Jesus on the cross did not change God's mind about sin — He hates sin today with just as holy hatred as He did before Calvary. The death of Jesus on the cross did not persuade an angry God to become a gracious God toward hell-deserving sinners. On the contrary, it was God's eternal grace that permitted the cross and the sufferings of His only begotten Son. Had there not first been grace, there would never have been a cross with its redeeming blood.

Dearly beloved, God is infinitely holy — He cannot be *unholy*. He cannot be tempted with evil (James 1:13); yet it was the infinitely holy God who manifested His great love by coming into this world in a body of flesh in the Person of the Lord Jesus Christ (II Cor. 5:19); and in that body of flesh He went to the cross, there taking upon Himself man's sin and condemnation. God in flesh so utterly dealt with sin and guilt to His own satisfaction and according to His own justice, that now the infinitely holy, just God can justify those who believe in Jesus.

"But now the righteousness of God without the law is manifested, being witnessed by the law and the prophets; Even the righteousness of God which is by faith of Jesus Christ unto all and upon all them that believe: for there is no difference: For all have sinned, and come short of the glory of God; Being justified freely by His grace through the redemption that is in Christ Jesus: Whom God hath set forth to be a propitiation through faith in His blood, to declare His righteousness for the remission of sins that are past, through the forbearance of God; to declare, I say, at this time His righteousness: that He might be just, and the justifier of him which believeth in Jesus. Where is boasting then? It is excluded. By what law? of works? Nay: but by the law of faith. Therefore we conclude that a man is justified by faith without the deeds of the law" (Rom. 3:21-28).

". . . God was in Christ, reconciling the world unto Himself . . ." (II Cor. 5:19). Jesus was none other than God wrapped up in flesh, reconciling the world *unto Himself*. What an infinitely holy God demanded, only an infinitely holy God could supply. God satisfied His holiness in the Lord Jesus Christ — and it all originated in God's grace.

"For He [God] hath made Him [Jesus] to be sin for us [for you and me] who knew no sin, that we [you and I] might be made the righteousness of God in Him [Jesus]" (II Cor. 5:21). My finite mind can comprehend neither the riches nor the depth of these words; but even though I do not fully understand them, *I believe them!*

"Take heed therefore unto yourselves, and to all the flock, over the which the Holy Ghost hath made you overseers, to feed the church of God, *which He hath purchased with His own blood*" (Acts 20:28).

In these Scriptures I read that the infinitely holy God made the spotless Son of God, the Lamb without spot or blemish, to be sin for me. Let us not soft-pedal the language; the Scriptures say *God MADE Him to be sin,* so let us read it as the Holy Spirit dictated it. *God made Jesus to be sin for me,* that I *in HIM* might be made the righteousness of God. Think on this, beloved; let its imprint be upon your heart: *IN JESUS the believer becomes the righteousness of God!* God purchased the Church (made up of all born again believers) with His own blood! Jesus received His flesh from the Virgin Mary, but He received His blood from the infinitely holy God. Jesus took our place, God laid our sins upon Him and He bore them to the cross and nailed them there. Thus, the righteousness of God, IN CHRIST, is reckoned to us who believe on Jesus.

Jesus on the cross was God's grace on display. Jesus on the cross was God *giving heaven's best for man's worst.* Jesus was not just "a good man" giving his life in martyrdom for a good cause — Jesus on the cross was GOD — suffering, paying the sin-debt, purchasing redemption for all. Jesus on the cross was God, in Christ, taking upon Himself all the sins of all men of all times, and atoning for sin in His death. Because of the atoning death of Jesus, God forgives sin and imputes righteousness. He reckons us righteous in His holy eyes, but this righteousness is made available to us ONLY because of the shed blood of Jesus.

Salvation is for *"whosoever"* — not by the philosophy of Jesus, nor by the example He set, nor through the holy, spotless life He lived — but by the shedding of His blood on the cross, where He was bruised, battered, and poured out *for us,* an offering for sin.

The heart of the Gospel message is. ". . . This is life eternal, that they might know thee the only true God, and Jesus Christ, whom thou hast sent" (John 17:3). And WHY was Jesus Christ sent? He answers that question Himself: "I have glorified thee on the earth: I have finished the work which thou gavest me to do" (John 17:4).

The crucifixion of the Lord Jesus Christ substantiates all prophecy: In Isaiah 53:4 and 12 it was prophesied, ". . . *He hath borne our griefs . . . He bare the sin of many.*" In the New Testament we read, "Who His own self bare our sins in His own body . . ." (I Pet. 2:24).

In Isaiah 53:4 it was prophesied, *"He carried our sorrows . . ."* John the Baptist announced, "Behold the Lamb of God, which taketh away the sin of the world" (John 1:29).

In Isaiah 53: 5 the prophecy is given, *"He was wounded for our transgressions . . ."* In John 19:37 we read, "They shall look on Him whom they pierced."

It was prophesied, *". . . He was bruised for our iniquities . . . it pleased the Lord to bruise Him"* (Isa. 53:5, 10). Peter declares, ". . . Christ hath once suffered for sins, the just for the unjust, that He might bring us to God" (I Pet. 3:18).

The prophet declared, *"The chastisement of our peace was upon Him . . ."* (Isa. 53:5). Paul announced that Christ "made peace by the blood of His cross . . ." (Col. 1:20).

The prophet prophesied, *". . . With His stripes we are healed"* (Isa. 53:5). Peter declares, ". . . By whose stripes ye *were* healed" (I Pet. 2:24).

In the words of the prophet, *". . . The Lord hath laid on Him the iniquity of us all"* (Isa. 53:6). Paul tells us that God "hath made HIM to be sin for us . . ." (II Cor. 5:21).

The death of Jesus on the cross was not just *an incident* in His life — it was the *purpose* of His life. The death of Jesus on the cross is the center and soul of all the graces, which the Holy Spirit, through the pen of Paul, summarizes as "Faith, Hope, and Charity [love]."

FAITH looks back to the cross of Jesus and sees Him there as our sin-bearer.

LOVE looks up to the throne of God and testifies, "He loved me, and gave Himself for me!"

HOPE looks beyond the cross — beyond the sufferings — to the glory, and sees the Lamb, seated at the right hand of God the Father. One day we will be with Him and in that glorious day we shall be *like Him!*

Faith rests upon the foundation of the finished work of Jesus. Just before He died He said, "It is finished." We *love* Him because He first loved us, and laid His life down for us on the cross. We look for *the blessed hope* and the glorious appearing of the great God and our Saviour, Jesus Christ.

It was God Himself who *provided* the atonement which
brought perfect satisfaction to Him. We must always remember
that God is a holy and righteous Ruler, as well as a loving and
merciful Father. It is true that God has a heart of love — God
IS love; but it is also true that He has a hand of righteousness,
and He cannot take part or have to do with anything *unrighteous.* God demonstrated His righteousness and holiness in the
death of the Lord Jesus Christ: He smote the Lamb, and in smit-
ing the Lamb He smote our sins in the *death* of the Lamb. He
did this in order to provide salvation.

In Christ, God satisfied justice; and that is the satisfaction
we have in our hearts when we believe on Jesus and trust in
His shed blood. We have peace, assurance, confidence. We no
longer have the spirit of fear, but rather the spirit of adoption
whereby we cry, "Abba, Father!"

2. *"Being . . . justified by His BLOOD."* The shed blood of
Jesus was the effect, not the cause, of God's love. Jesus hanging
on the cross displayed God's love as being consistent with God's
righteousness. God IN CHRIST completely met every require-
ment of God's throne, that He might provide redemption consistent with His holy and righteous nature. Therefore, the believer rests upon God's justice for salvation.

Centuries before the cross, Jehovah God said, ". . . The life
of the flesh is in the blood: and I have given it to you upon the
altar to make an atonement for your souls: for it is the blood
that maketh an atonement for the soul" (Lev. 17:11). To me,
the outstanding statement in the New Testament concerning
the blood of Christ is found in Hebrews 9:22: ". . . *Without
shedding of blood is no remission."*

Following is a summary of verses pointing to the blood that
brings redemption and cleansing:

Luke 22:20, Hebrews 10:29: The blood of the new covenant.

Hebrews 10:19: The blood of Jesus.

Acts 20:28: The blood of God.

I Peter 1:2: The blood of Jesus Christ.

Romans 3:24, 25: The blood of Christ Jesus, "whom God
hath set forth to be a propitiation through faith in His blood . . ."

I John 1:7: The blood of Jesus Christ, God's Son.

Hebrews 9:14: The blood of Christ.

I Corinthians 11:27: The blood of the Lord.

The Lord Jesus Christ, while here upon earth, frequently emphasized the necessity for the shedding of His blood:

"For this is MY BLOOD of the new testament, which is shed for many for the remission of sins" (Matt. 26:28).

"And He said unto them, This is MY BLOOD of the new testament, which is shed for many" (Mark 14:24).

". . . This cup is the new testament in MY BLOOD, which is shed for you" (Luke 22:20).

"Whoso eateth my flesh, and drinketh MY BLOOD, hath eternal life; and I will raise him up at the last day. For my flesh is meat indeed, and MY BLOOD is drink indeed. He that eateth my flesh, and drinketh MY BLOOD, dwelleth in me, and I in him" (John 6:54-56).

After the Day of Pentecost, the Holy Spirit frequently speaks of the blessings of the shed blood of the Lord Jesus Christ, using the terms, "HIS OWN blood . . . HIS blood." Study Acts 20:28; Romans 3:25; 5:9; Ephesians 1:7; Colossians 1:14; Hebrews 9:12; 13:12; Revelation 1:5; 5:9.

> There is a fountain filled with blood
> Drawn from Immanuel's veins;
> And sinners, plunged beneath that flood,
> Lose all their guilty stains.

3. *"Being justified by FAITH"* The third aspect of justification is by faith in the finished work of Jesus — not by works which WE are able to do, but by the work which HE completed and announced to the heavenly Father as finished (John 19:30).

"Therefore by the deeds of the law there shall no flesh be justified in His sight: for by the law is the knowledge of sin" (Rom. 3:20).

Romans 3:22 speaks of "the righteousness of God which is *by faith* of Jesus Christ unto all and upon all them that believe . . ."

"But to Him that worketh not, but *believeth* on Him that justifieth the ungodly, his *faith* is counted for righteousness" (Rom. 4:5).

"For by grace are ye saved through faith; and that not of yourselves: it is the gift of God: Not of works, lest any man should boast" (Eph. 2:8, 9).

By the eternal grace of God, through the shed blood of the Lamb of God, salvation for the sinner became possible; but it is by our faith in the finished work of Jesus that salvation becomes ours personally. What Jesus procured on the cross through the shedding of His blood, our faith secures in our own hearts when we place our trust in what He has done *for* us. We are justified only on the ground of the shed blood of the Lamb of God when we exercise faith in His finished work. The blood has been shed, the atonement has been made, the ransom has been paid in full — but all of this will profit us nothing unless we exercise simple, childlike faith in the finished work of the Lord Jesus Christ.

Tens of thousands of poor souls are stumbling into hell over the very simplicity of salvation. To receive Jesus Christ simply by faith leaves no room for self-satisfaction or pride; they would much prefer to be asked to do something spectacular or outstanding, something that would place emphasis on their own efforts and accomplishments. They refuse to receive and believe the simple Word of God: *"Believe on the Lord Jesus Christ, and thou shalt be saved."* To many, this is entirely too easy, too cheap; it is not enough. They want to DO something, GIVE something, BE something. But the Bible makes it crystal-clear that salvation is the gift of God:

"For ye see your calling, brethren, how that not many wise men after the flesh, not many mighty, not many noble, are called: But God hath chosen the foolish things of the world to confound the wise; and God hath chosen the weak things of the world to confound the things which are mighty; and base things of the world, and things which are despised, hath God chosen, yea, and things which are not, to bring to nought things that are: That no flesh should glory in His presence. But of Him are ye in Christ Jesus, who of God is made unto us wisdom, and righteousness, and sanctification, and redemption; that, according as it is written, He that glorieth, let him glory in the Lord" (I Cor. 1:26-31).

If man can do anything to save himself, then the death of Jesus on the cross was unnecessary; but there is *not one single thing* that man can do to save himself, nor is there anything he can do to *add to* the finished work of Jesus which makes salvation possible.

Many people confuse *faith* with "feelings." What IS faith? The Word of God tells us that *"faith is the substance of things hoped for, the evidence of things not seen"* (Heb. 11:1). Faith is believing what God says, simply *because God said it* — and God cannot lie.

God said, "Come, and I will give you rest," and when we come to Him, He GIVES rest, regardless of how we may feel or act. There are those who weep when they are saved. Others laugh, still others show no outward emotion at all. But neither reaction nor emotional stir have anything to do with saving faith. *Faith believes God,* as did Abraham, whose faith was "counted unto him for righteousness." The only way to do business with God, and the only way to obtain anything FROM God, is *by faith.*

"But without faith it is impossible to please Him: for he that cometh to God must believe that He is, and that He is a rewarder of them that diligently seek Him" (Heb. 11:6).

There are those who are afraid that they do not have *enough* faith. But beloved, faith does not come in inches, feet, or yards. Faith is not measured in ounces or pounds. *If you have any faith at all,* you have enough faith to be saved. It is not the *amount* of faith that is important, but *IN WHOM do you HAVE your faith?* The all-important question is, "What think ye of *Christ?* Whose Son is He?"

Paul puts it in these words: ". . . If thou shalt confess with thy mouth the Lord Jesus, and shalt believe in thine heart that God hath raised Him from the dead, thou shalt be saved. For with the heart man believeth unto righteousness; and with the mouth confession is made unto salvation" (Rom. 10:9, 10).

To believe with the heart means much more than believing that God is good, and that Jesus was His Son. To believe with the heart goes much deeper than "head belief." In the Word of God, *the heart* stands for "'the inner man." Thus, *to believe with the heart* is to believe with *the entire being*. "Heart belief" involves trust and surrender.

Saving faith looks beyond that which is finite: it looks beyond the present to the eternal and the divine. True faith is never occupied with itself, nor with "feelings." The object of true faith is the Lord Jesus Christ. IN HIM faith finds salvation from sin. Faith RESTS in Him, as the ivy vine clings to the oak and lives upon it.

Faith is the *feet* which walk to Jesus simply because He invites, "Come unto me, all ye that labour and are heavy laden, and I will give you rest" (Matt. 11:28).

Faith is the *hand* which receives the Gift of God: ". . . As many as RECEIVED Him, to them gave He power to become the sons of God, even to them that believe on His name" (John 1:12).

Faith is the *sense* which tastes and sees that the Lord is gracious (I Pet. 2:3).

Faith is the *eye* which looks to the Lord Jesus Christ and thereby proves the truth of His words: "Look unto me, and be ye saved, all the ends of the earth: for I am God, and there is none else" (Isa. 45:22).

Faith is the *touch* which comes in contact with the Lord Jesus Christ and finds the healing power of His saving grace (Mark 5:29-34).

Faith is the *ear* which listens, hears the voice of Jesus, and obeys His Word: "*My sheep hear my voice*, and I know them, and they follow me" (John 10:27). "Verily, verily, I say unto you, *He that heareth my Word*, and believeth on Him that sent me, hath everlasting life, and shall not come into condemnation; but is passed from death unto life" (John 5:24).

Faith does not look for evidence — either in feelings or circumstances around us. True faith rests on something altogether apart from these.

Faith is not effort. We exercise true faith when we cease to try to do for ourselves, and rest in perfect confidence in God's ability to do FOR us. When we depend upon HIM to do for us what we know we cannot do for ourselves, and when we cease trying to *help* Him do it, we will then have perfect peace and rest, instead of being plagued with worry and anxiety.

To exercise true faith in God is to rely upon His character and His promise, trusting in Him and in His Word. "Faithful is He who has promised." He said He would save us — and He will!

Someone may ask, "How do I know that my faith is genuine? How do I know that I have *true faith?*" The answer is found in the Word of God:

James 2:14-17: "What doth it profit, my brethren, though a man say he hath faith, and have not works? Can faith save him? If a brother or sister be naked, and destitute of daily food, and one of you say unto them, Depart in peace, be ye warmed and filled; notwithstanding ye give them not those things which are needful to the body; what doth it profit? Even so faith, if it hath not works, is dead, being alone."

James 2:24, 26: "Ye see then how that by works a man is justified, and not by faith only . . . for as the body without the spirit is dead, so faith without works is dead also."

The person who professes faith in God, and yet produces no good works, has a *counterfeit faith.* The Word of God clearly teaches that we are justified BY FAITH ALONE — faith minus works; but the faith that saves is faith that *works.* Faith *without* works is dead faith.

"For we are HIS workmanship, created in Christ Jesus UNTO GOOD WORKS, which God hath before ordained that we should walk in them" (Eph. 2:10). The grace of God that brings salvation teaches us to be *zealous* unto good works, anxious to do good works for Christ's sake. Works do not justify the believer, but true faith proves its reality IN WORKS. There is no contradiction between the Gospel Paul preached, and the teaching of James. Paul emphasizes the divine fact that *salvation cannot be earned* — it is by grace, through faith, plus nothing. James emphasizes that salvation *causes* us to work, puts within us a desire to work, because we are alive unto God, *created IN CHRIST JESUS unto good works.*

Someone has said that *faith and works* can be compared to a railroad track, where two rails run side by side, both rails being imperative if the train is to reach its destination. If one rail is missing, the train will surely meet with disaster. In the same

way, *true faith produces works, and faith without works is dead.*
Examine yourself, and see if you be in THE faith.

The Results of Justification

It would be humanly impossible to measure the length,
breadth, and depth of justification. The finite mind of man
could never comprehend the measure of the tremendous blessings which are ours when we are justified by faith in the shed
blood of the Lamb of God. From Paul's epistles to the several
different churches, we grasp but a meagre conception of the
measure of justification, but its full measure and benefits will
not be known this side of heaven.

To the believers in Rome, Paul gave seven specific results of
justification:

1. "Therefore being justified by faith, we have PEACE
with God through our Lord Jesus Christ: By whom also we have
access by faith into this grace wherein we stand, and rejoice in
hope of the glory of God.

"And not only so, but we glory in tribulations also: knowing
that tribulation worketh patience; and patience, experience;
and experience, hope; and hope maketh not ashamed; because
the love of God is shed abroad in our hearts by the Holy Ghost
which is given unto us.

"For when we were yet without strength, in due time Christ
died for the ungodly. For scarcely for a righteous man will one
die: yet peradventure for a good man some would even dare
to die. But God commendeth His love toward us, in that, while
we were yet sinners, Christ died for us.

"Much more then, being now justified by His blood, we shall
be saved from wrath through Him. For if, when we were
enemies, we were reconciled to God by the death of His Son,
much more, being reconciled, we shall be saved by His life.
And not only so, but we also joy in God through our Lord Jesus
Christ, by whom we have now received the atonement" (Rom.
5:1-11).

Being justified by faith, we automatically have peace with
God. We also have access into His grace. We stand in the grace
of God. We have joy, we rejoice in the hope of the glory of God.

We glory in tribulation for we know that "tribulation worketh patience" and is profitable to us. Patience results in experience, experience brings greater hope — and hope causes us not to be ashamed, because the love of God is in us, shed abroad in our hearts by the Holy Ghost. Thus, the believer, having peace with God, is justified before God, and there is no accusation against us:

"WHO shall lay anything to the charge of God's elect? *It is God that justifieth*" (Rom. 8:33). No one in heaven or in earth can bring any accusation against the believer. Justification by the blood of Jesus puts to silence all accusers. Satan's mouth is stopped, and even the conscience that would condemn us is silenced. "If our heart condemn us not, then have we confidence toward God" (I John 3:21). Therefore, being justified by faith in the shed blood of the Lamb of God, the Christian possesses peace with God.

2. The believer possesses a JOY that is unspeakable and full of glory, because all condemnation is removed: "Who is he that condemneth?" (Rom. 8:34). The answer to that question is found in Romans 8:1: "There IS therefore now NO CONDEMNATION to them which are IN CHRIST JESUS . . ."

John 3:18 tells us, *"He that believeth on Him is NOT condemned*: but he that believeth not is condemned already, because he hath not believed in the name of the only begotten Son of God."

For the believer, condemnation and judgment are past. Sin has already been *judged and punished* in the death of Christ. He is not *bearing* our sins, He is not *going to bear our sins* at some future date; but He BORE our sins in His own body on the cross, and He is our security against condemnation. . . . *UNLESS* . . . unless the death of Jesus ceases to satisfy the holiness and the righteousness of God, unless our Mediator, our Advocate, ceases to satisfy God regarding those who believe in His finished work, *none in heaven or in earth can condemn the justified believer, for he is saved and secured in the shed blood through the finished work of Jesus.*

3. The born again believer possesses peace WITH God, joy IN God, and he also possesses HOPE, because none can separate

The Gospel of Grace

him *from* God:

"Who shall separate us from the love of Christ? Shall tribulation, or distress, or persecution, or famine, or nakedness, or peril, or sword? As it is written, For thy sake we are killed all the day long; we are accounted as sheep for the slaughter. Nay, in all these things we are more than conquerors through Him that loved us. *For I am persuaded, that neither death, nor life, nor angels, nor principalities, nor powers, nor things present, nor things to come, nor height, nor depth, nor any other creature, shall be able to separate us from the love of God, which is in Christ Jesus our Lord"* (Rom. 8:35-39).

". . . After that the kindness and love of God our Saviour toward man appeared, not by works of righteousness which we have done, but accordng to His mercy He saved us, by the washing of regeneration, and renewing of the Holy Ghost; which He shed on us abundantly through Jesus Christ our Saviour; THAT BEING JUSTIFIED BY HIS GRACE, WE SHOULD BE MADE HEIRS ACCORDING TO THE HOPE OF ETERNAL LIFE" (Tit. 3:4-7).

According to the Gospel dictated to the Apostle Paul by the Holy Ghost, believers are NOT condemned, they cannot BE condemned, because they are justified by the blood, in the name of the Lord Jesus Christ who satisfied God's holiness and righteousness.

Even when we were enemies to God — wicked, lost, hopeless and without strength, dead in trespasses and sin — *Christ died* for the ungodly! Even though sin brought us under the condemnation of a holy God, through faith in the finished work of the Lord Jesus Christ we can become sons of God, accepted by Him. Through justification, our hearts can be made pure, filled with peace, joy unspeakable and full of glory.

I have peace because there is none to accuse.

I have joy because there is none to condemn.

I have hope because there is nought that can separate me from the love of God. I am His, He bought me, He paid the purchase price of my redemption. He justified me through the shed blood of the spotless Lamb. I am His and He is mine — forever and forever!

Chapter V

The Believer and Adoption

Four great Bible words make up the foursquare foundation
of the Christian experience:

1. Forgiveness
2. Justification
3. Regeneration
4. Adoption

Upon these four tremendous "Gospel stones" rests the whole
of the Christian life, from start to finish. We are forgiven,
justified, regenerated, and adopted instantaneously when we
exercise faith in the finished work of Jesus, and yet these words
are not synonymous.

Forgiveness has to do with the putting away of sins: "To
the praise of the glory of His grace, wherein He hath made us
accepted in the beloved. In whom we have redemption through
His blood, *the forgiveness of sins,* according to the riches of
His grace" (Eph. 1:6, 7).

"Giving thanks unto the Father, which hath made us meet
to be partakers of the inheritance of the saints in light:
who hath delivered us from the power of darkness, and hath
translated us into the kingdom of His dear Son: in whom we
have redemption through His blood, *even the forgiveness of
sins*" (Col. 1:12-14).

We can forgive another who has wronged us, we can forgive
our friends when they trespass against us — and as born again
believers we must even forgive our enemies; but forgiveness is
as far as man can go. We can *forgive* those who trespass against
us, but we can never *justify* one who trespasses against another.

Through the shed blood of His cross Jesus made forgiveness

possible. When we believe on Jesus, God the Father forgives us
and puts away our sins because the sin-debt has been settled
through the one offering made by Jesus on the cross. When we
repent of our sins, God forgives us for Christ's sake:

". . . Be ye kind one to another, tenderhearted, forgiving one
another, even as God *for Christ's sake* hath forgiven you"
(Eph. 4:32).

"I write unto you, little children, because *your sins are forgiven
you for His name's sake*" (I John 2:12).

Justification goes much deeper and has a much broader
meaning than forgiveness. Justification is more than pardon — it
puts upon us *perfect righteousness.* The governor of the state
can (and does) pardon prisoners, but neither the governor, the
president, nor anyone else can justify a criminal for the crime
committed.

There is no just reason for a person committing a crime
against his fellowman. Therefore, justification goes further than
forgiveness (or pardon). God not only *forgives* our sins, He
also puts upon us His perfect righteousness:

"For what saith the Scripture? Abraham believed God, and
it was counted unto him for righteousness . . . Even as David
also describeth the blessedness of the man, unto whom God
imputeth righteousness without works, saying, Blessed are they
whose iniquities are forgiven, and whose sins are covered.
Blessed is the man to whom the Lord will not impute sin"
(Rom. 4:3, 6-8).

To *justify* means to completely exonerate, vindicate, acquit.
I confess that this glorious truth is too wonderful for me, my
finite mind cannot comprehend the riches and glory of it all;
but I know that the moment I placed my faith in the shed
blood and the finished work of Jesus, *God acquitted me because
of my faith* in the shed blood and Christ's finished work, and
put within me and upon me *the perfect righteousness of
Jesus Christ!* I do not profess to *understand* it, but it is the
Word of God and *I believe it.* It is only through faith in the shed
blood of Jesus that my sins have been forgiven, and I possess
the perfect righteousness of God.

Regeneration puts Divine nature within us. God forgives our sins for Christ's sake, He justifies us and puts upon us the perfect righteousness of Christ, but He also gives us a new nature:

"Not by works of righteousness which we have done, but according to His mercy He saved us, *by the washing of regeneration,* and renewing of the Holy Ghost" (Tit. 3:5).

"Whereby are given unto us exceeding great and precious promises: that by these ye might be *partakers of the divine nature,* having escaped the corruption that is in the world through lust" (II Pet. 1:4).

We are not regenerated through works, good living, generous giving, nor by abstaining. We are regenerated through *the washing of regeneration,* and the renewing of the Holy Spirit.

When we exercise faith in the finished work of Jesus, God puts within us the Holy Spirit:

Jesus said to Nicodemus, "Verily, verily, I say unto thee, Except a man be born of water *and of the Spirit,* he cannot enter into the kingdom of God" (John 3:5).

"So then they that are in the flesh cannot please God. But ye are not in the flesh, but in the Spirit, if so be that the Spirit of God dwell in you. Now if any man have not the Spirit of Christ, he is none of His . . . For as many as are led by the Spirit of God, they are the sons of God. . . . The Spirit [Himself] beareth witness with our spirit, that we are the children of God" (Rom. 8:8-16 in part).

It is wonderful to know that we are forgiven for Christ's sake. It is glorious to know that we are justified, and that we have within and upon us the perfect righteousness of God. But it is even more glorious to know that God lives in us in the Person of the Holy Spirit, and we have a new heart, a new spirit, a new nature:

"*Therefore if any man be in Christ, he is a new creature: old things are passed away; behold, ALL THINGS are become new*" (II Cor. 5:17).

Adoption places us in a new position in our relationship to God the Father. In the dictionary we read that *adoption* means "to take as one's own what is not so *naturally* . . . to take a person into a particular relationship, as of an heir . . . to take voluntarily a child of other parents as one's own child." Adoption,

then, has to do with heirship, position, status. The believer's
relation to God as a son results from the new birth (John 1:12,
13) whereas *adoption* is the act of God whereby a child is placed
in the *position* of an adult son — an heir. *All born again believers are* adopted into the family of God!

Only in the epistles of Paul do we find the word "adoption."
It is mentioned five times in Paul's writings: We find it in Romans 8:15, 23; 9:4; Ephesians 1:5; and Galatians 4:5.

The greater part of the Gospel preached by Paul is directed
to born again believers. I am not suggesting that there is not
salvation Gospel in his epistles, for certainly he gives the plan
of salvation and tells us that we are saved by grace through
faith, making it plain that "with the heart man believeth unto
righteousness"; but the heart of his message is to "the born
ones."

Forgiveness puts away our sins, *justification* puts within us
perfect righteousness, *regeneration* makes us partakers of the
Divine nature, and *adoption* places us in a new position in our
relationship to God the Father, making us heirs of God, joint-
heirs with Jesus Christ.

Therefore, believers are not just "disciples," we are not just
followers or friends of God. *We are His sons and daughters,
children of the Lord God Almighty!* God has not only forgiven
us, delivered us from the prison of sin and set us free from
condemnation and guilt, accounted us righteous and imparted
to us Divine nature (His own life), but He has now *adopted us*
into the royal family of heaven. We have a seat at His royal
table, with all the privileges and rights of His royal children!

Adoption Affords Specific Blessings

Having been brought into a position of sonship through the
miracle of the new birth, and adopted into the family of God,
the believer has certain and specific blessings:

"For as many as are led by the Spirit of God, they are the
sons of God. For ye have not received the spirit of bondage
again to fear; but ye have received the Spirit of adoption, whereby we cry, Abba, Father. The Spirit itself beareth witness with
our spirit, that we are the children of God" (Rom. 8:14-16).

In John 8:32, 36 Jesus tells us that the believer is *set free*. Now Paul adds that the born again ones do not receive the spirit of bondage, but rather *"the Spirit of adoption* whereby we cry Abba, Father." Notice that the word "Spirit" in this latter phrase is capitalized, denoting Deity — the HOLY SPIRIT.

Thus, the believer is born into God's family, adopted as a full-grown child with all bondage taken away. We are free — and we have no fear, because God is our Father. And in verse 16 we are assured that the Holy Spirit *bears witness* with OUR spirit (in our hearts) that we ARE children of God.

In Romans 8:14 Paul speaks of "the *sons* of God." In verses 17 and 21 of the same chapter he speaks of "the *children* of God." "Two Greek words are used here — *teknon* (v. 14) meaning "one born, *a child*," and *huios*, meaning "sons." Here we have babyhood and sonhood contrasted. When one is born again, he is but a *babe* in Christ. Therefore, Peter admonishes, "As newborn babes, desire the sincere milk of the Word, *that ye may grow thereby*" (I Pet. 2:2). But even though we are babes in Christ when we are born again, we are nevertheless adopted into God's family with the position of full heirship.

"And because ye are sons, God hath sent forth the Spirit of His Son into your hearts, crying, Abba, Father. Wherefore thou art no more a servant, but a son; and if a son, then an heir of God through Christ" (Gal. 4:6, 7). Christianity teaches that the Holy Spirit indwells every born again believer. No other religion on earth teaches this doctrine. Christianity is CHRIST IN YOU in the Person of the Holy Spirit.

Every believer possesses Christ in His entirety; *we are complete IN HIM.* In Him we find our sufficiency. IN HIM every need is fully met. IN HIM we live, and move, and have our being. We are *indwelt* by the Holy Spirit, *led* by the Holy Spirit, *assured* by the Holy Spirit, *filled* with the Holy Spirit, and *sealed* by the Holy Spirit until the day of redemption, when the Spirit (that raised up Christ from the dead) will also quicken the mortal body of the believer. Even the least among the saints can say with Paul, "I am crucified with Christ: nevertheless I live; *yet not I, but Christ liveth in me*: and the life which I now live in the flesh, I live by the faith of the Son of

God who loved me and gave Himself for me" (Gal. 2:20).
"CHRIST LIVETH IN ME!" is the testimony of every born
again believer.

Believers enjoy the real, personal presence of Jesus — not
His presence communicated in the sacrament of bread and the
fruit of the vine, not His presence in the holy of holies behind
the veil — but *He lives IN US.* We are the temple of the
Holy Ghost:

"What? Know ye not that your body is the temple of the
Holy Ghost which is in you, which ye have of God, and ye are
not your own?" (I Cor. 6:19).

We know the Heavenly Father who loves and cares for
His own:

"Like as a father pitieth His children, so the Lord pitieth them
that fear Him. For He knoweth our frame; He remembereth
that we are dust" (Psa. 103:13, 14).

"Blessed be God, even the Father of our Lord Jesus Christ,
the Father of mercies, and the God of all comfort" (II Cor. 1:3).

We have the same assurance given by the Lord Jesus to His
disciples: ". . . Your Father knoweth what things ye have need
of, before ye ask Him" (Matt. 6:8). "Are not two sparrows sold
for a farthing? and one of them shall not fall on the ground
without your Father. But the very hairs of your head are all
numbered. Fear ye not therefore, ye are of more value than
many sparrows" (Matt. 10:29-31).

We have a loving Father who is concerned about our every
interest and personal need. He cares for us and makes loving
provision for every minute detail of our living. These glorious
provisions are included in the position and privileges afforded
by our adoption.

The Purpose of the Holy Spirit in Our Lives

The Holy Spirit *convicts us of sin and draws us to God:*

"No man can come to me, except the Father which hath sent
me draw him . . ." (John 6:44).

"Nevertheless I tell you the truth; It is expedient for you that
I go away: for if I go not away, the Comforter will not come
unto you; but if I depart, I will send Him unto you. And when

He is come, He will reprove the world of sin, and of righteousness, and of judgment: Of sin, because they believe not on me; of righteousness, because I go to my Father, and ye see me no more; of judgment, because the prince of this world is judged" (John 16:7-11).

We are *born of the Spirit*:

"Jesus answered, Verily, verily, I say unto thee, Except a man be born of water and of the Spirit, he cannot enter into the kingdom of God. That which is born of the flesh is flesh; and that which is born of the Spirit is spirit" (John 3:5, 6).

We are *led by the Spirit*:

"For as many as are led by the Spirit of God, they are the sons of God" (Rom. 8:14).

We are *assured by the Spirit*:

"The Spirit (Himself) beareth witness with our spirit, that we are the children of God" (Rom. 8:16).

We are *sealed by the Spirit*:

"And grieve not the Holy Spirit of God, whereby ye are sealed unto the day of redemption" (Eph. 4:30).

But the Spirit does more than this. The divine purpose of His indwelling the life of the believer is, above all else, to conform the believer into the image of Christ, Himself the image of the invisible God:

"For whom He did foreknow, He also did predestinate to be conformed to the image of His Son, that He might be the firstborn among many brethren" (Rom. 8:29).

"Giving thanks unto the Father . . . who hath translated us into the kingdom of His dear Son . . . who is the image of the invisible God, the firstborn of every creature" (Col. 1:12-15 in part).

Jesus in the flesh revealed the Father, and from within the believer the Holy Spirit manifests and forms the adopted child into the image of Christ. Paul wrote to the Galatian Christians, "My little children, of whom I travail in birth again until Christ be formed in you" (Gal. 4:19).

The burden of Paul's heart was that his *children* in the faith become *full grown* in the faith. He wanted them to be everything they were supposed to be (and *could* be) *for* Christ,

IN Christ, through the power of the Spirit. Of himself he said, "For the law of the Spirit of life in Christ Jesus hath made me free from the law of sin and death" (Rom. 8:2).

The believer is set free from the slavery and servitude of sin. Every believer has the assurance of Philippians 4:13: "I can do all things through Christ which strengtheneth me."

Every believer has the promise, ". . . Sin shall not have dominion over you: for ye are not under law, but under grace" (Rom. 6:14).

Every believer can give testimony, "We are more than conquerors through Him that loved us" (Rom. 8:37).

We become born again believers by God's grace — but His grace does not stop there. Paul tells us, "For the grace of God that bringeth salvation hath appeared to all men, teaching us that, denying ungodliness and worldly lusts, we should live soberly, righteously, and godly, in this present world; looking for that blessed hope, and the glorious appearing of the great God and our Saviour Jesus Christ; who gave Himself for us, that He might redeem us from all iniquity, and purify unto Himself a peculiar people, zealous of good works" (Tit. 2:11-14).

The grace of God brings salvation — and then sets up a classroom in our hearts (in the inner man) and instructs us to deny ungodliness and worldly lusts, to live sober, righteous, godly lives in this present world, and to look for that glorious event when the great God and our Saviour Jesus Christ will call us to meet Him in the air.

Christ gave Himself for us, paid the sin-debt to redeem us from all iniquity, purify us, and make of us *"a peculiar people, ZEALOUS OF GOOD WORKS."* In Ephesians 2:10 Paul tells us, ". . . We are His workmanship, created in Christ Jesus unto good works, which God hath before ordained that we should walk in them." We have within us the power and the motive to assure us of victory and reward.

In I John 5:4, 5, we read, "For whatsoever [whosoever] is born of God overcometh the world: and this is the victory that overcometh the world, even our faith. Who is he that overcometh the world, but he that believeth that Jesus is the Son of God?"

There is no suggestion that we *may* overcome, or that there is a *possibility or chance* that we can overcome. The statement is clear and positive: *"Whosoever is born of God OVERCOM-ETH the world!"*

Then, in Romans 8:26, 27 we read, "Likewise the Spirit also helpeth our infirmities: for we know not what we should pray for as we ought: but the Spirit itself maketh intercession for us with groanings which cannot be uttered. And He that searcheth the hearts knoweth what is the mind of the Spirit, because He maketh intercession for the saints according to the will of God."

The only safe, profitable, and right road for the believer to travel is the pathway of the will of God — and if we *do not know* the will of God but WANT to know it, the Holy Spirit helps us and prays in our stead, "with groanings which cannot be uttered," and God the Father understands.

How glorious to know that believers are possessors of the Holy Spirit, that we are adopted into the family of God, with all the privileges and blessings of that position, and that we are members of the family of heaven.

Our Assurance of Heavenly Riches in Glory

"But when the fulness of the time was come, God sent forth His Son, made of a woman, made under the law, to redeem them that were under the law, that we might receive the adoption of sons. And because ye are sons, God hath sent forth the Spirit of His Son into your hearts, crying, Abba, Father. *Wherefore thou art no more a servant, but a son; and if a son, then an heir of God through Christ"* (Gal. 4:4-7).

I wonder if we really understand these tremendous words? Not only are we heirs of God the Father, but He has placed us right alongside the Son of His love — Jesus Christ our Lord; and to be a joint-heir with Christ can mean only one thing: It can only mean that we are to share in the glories and the riches of the Father in the same manner as the only begotten Son shares God's riches and glories. This will be our portion throughout the unending day in the Pearly White City. It is all too wonderful for me! I cannot understand it, but I do thank God

for it — and I know it is true, because God said it, and God cannot lie!

Paul's letter to the Romans contains an encouraging and
enlightening promise. We know that the whole creation was
cursed when Adam sinned. ". . . The creature was made subject
to vanity, not willingly, but by reason of Him who hath sub-
jected the same in hope. Because the creature itself also
*shall be delivered from the bondage of corruption into the
glorious liberty of the children of God.* For we know that the
whole creation groaneth and travaileth in pain together until
now. And not only they, but ourselves also, which have the
firstfruits of the Spirit, even we ourselves groan within ourselves,
waiting for the adoption, to wit, *the redemption of our body.*
For we are saved by hope: but hope that is seen is not hope:
for what a man seeth, why doth he yet hope for? But if
we hope for that we see not, then do we with patience wait
for it" (Rom. 8:20-25).

One grand and glorious day, ALL CREATION will be
delivered from the curse. Even those of us who have "the
firstfruits" groan and travail in these bodies of corruption,
waiting FOR THE REDEMPTION OF OUR BODIES. One
day, we will receive our glorified bodies, like unto the body
of Christ, now seated at the right hand of God the Father:
". . . We know that when He shall appear, *we shall be like Him;*
for we shall see Him as He is" (I John 3:2).

Let us hear the testimony of Peter concerning our position
as heirs of God and joint-heirs with Christ:

"Blessed be the God and Father of our Lord Jesus Christ,
which according to His abundant mercy hath begotten us again
unto a lively hope by the resurrection of Jesus Christ from the
dead, *to an inheritance incorruptible, and undefiled,* and that
fadeth not away, reserved in heaven for you, who are kept by
the power of God through faith unto salvation ready to be
revealed in the last time" (I Pet. 1:3-5).

What a promise! What an inheritance to look forward to — an
inheritance incorruptible, undefiled, spotless, pure as God's
righteousness, an inheritance that "fadeth not away." Our inheritance will never tarnish nor cease to be. It is safe, because

it is "reserved in heaven." When we reach that land that is fairer than day we will come into full possession of our eternal inheritance.

When Did All of This Begin?

. Before God laid the foundation of this earth, before He created the dust out of which He formed Adam, He planned and perfected — not only our complete salvation, but His plan for the ages of ages:

"According as He hath chosen us in Him *before the foundation of the world,* that we should be holy and without blame before Him in love; having predestinated us unto the adoption of children by Jesus Christ to Himself, according to the good pleasure of His will, to the praise of the glory of His grace, wherein He hath made us *accepted in the Beloved*" (Eph. 1:4-6).

The incarnation of Jesus was foreordained from eternity. He was slain before the foundation of the world, and in the same way, at the same time, God foreordained that we be adopted into the family of heaven, enjoying all the privileges of His own beloved, only begotten Son.

In the fulness of the time, God sent forth His Son (Gal. 4:4) that we might receive the adoption of sons. "And He is the propitiation for our sins: and not for our's only, but also for the sins of the whole world" (I John 2:2).

The glorious blessings and privileges which are ours as sons of God became ours "through the redemption that is in Christ Jesus" (Rom. 3:24).

Scholars tell us that in the New Testament Greek there are three words which explain the full meaning of our one word "redemption." The first Greek word signifies "to buy in the slave market." The second Greek word means, *"to buy out from* the slave market," and the third Greek word means "freedom after paying the price of ransom." In Paul's day, a slave could be bought and then re-sold to another master in the same market on the same day; or, he could be bought and taken out of the market by the one who bought him; or, he could be bought and then *set free* by the purchaser.

Our redemption through the shed blood of the Lord Jesus Christ includes all three. Unbelievers are slaves of sin, sold under sin (Rom. 7:14) in the slave markets of the world. Jesus our Saviour took a body of flesh, and by His incarnation He came into the world to purchase our redemption, to pay the ransom price. He did that, and more:

By His blood shed on the cross, He redeemed us "from this present evil world, according to the will of God and our Father" (Gal. 1:4). Then, having paid the tremendous price that no one else *could* have ever paid, thereby having purchased our redemption, Christ in us in the Person of the Holy Spirit has *emancipated* us and set us free! He has broken the power of sin in our lives. We are no longer the *victims of sin* — we are *victors OVER sin!*

In the by-and-by (no man knows the day or the hour) Jesus will come and set our *bodies* free! In His death on the cross He has already delivered us from the *penalty* of sin. Abiding in our hearts in the Person of the Holy Spirit He daily sets us free from the *power* and pollution of sin. But in that great day just ahead of us, He will come to deliver us from the very *presence* of sin, and we will be caught out of this world to meet Him in the clouds in the air, never to look upon sin again! What a glorious salvation: Every true believer should pray with John the Beloved, "Even so, COME, Lord Jesus!"

Christians Bear the Heavenly Father's Name

All believers are children in the family of God, and as such, we bear His name — a grand and glorious privilege, but also involving grave and weighty responsibilities and obligations.

"For this cause I bow my knees unto the Father of our Lord Jesus Christ, *of whom the whole family in heaven and earth is named*" (Eph. 3:14, 15).

". . . Ye are sanctified . . . ye are justified *in the name of the Lord Jesus*, and by the Spirit of our God" (I Cor. 6:11).

The greater the name, the greater the sin and shame if that name is dishonored, and we bear the greatest of ALL names: Christian (which means Christ-like). A sinful, indifferent world that will not read the Bible will think of Christ in accordance with the way we live — the things we do, what we say, the places we go and the company we keep. In all things the Christian should glorify the Lord Jesus Christ and magnify His name. "Whether therefore ye eat, or drink, or whatsoever ye do, do all to the glory of God" (I Cor. 10:31). We who bear the name of Jesus have no personal right to do anything that would bring shame or reproach upon that name!

One of the grievances against the believers in Galatia was that after having been redeemed by the blood of the Lamb and set free by the grace of God, they were leaning again toward the very bondage from which they had been set free. Paul admonished them, "But now, after that ye have known God, or rather are known OF God, how turn ye again to the weak and beggarly elements, whereunto ye desire again to be in bondage? . . . So then, brethren, we are not children of the bondwoman, but of the free . . . Stand fast therefore in the liberty wherewith Christ hath made us free, and be not entangled again with the yoke of bondage" (Gal. 4:9, 31; 5:1).

This admonition follows closely after Paul's dissertation on the adoption of believers into the family of God. As children of God, Christians are to stand steadfast in the liberty wherewith Christ has made us free, and make no provision or plans to return to the bondage of the old life. Old habits, old friends, old pleasures and pastimes must be forever ignored and forsaken. They belong to the life from which we have been redeemed, out of which we have been adopted into the family of heaven.

We read in Luke 17:32, "REMEMBER LOT'S WIFE!" Why would the Holy Spirit have us remember Lot's wife? The only reasonable answer is that Lot's wife would not cut loose from her friends and possessions in Sodom. She was safely outside the city — *but she turned and looked back!* Christians are made free indeed, for the Son has made us free (John 8:36). We should never entertain a thought of returning to the bondage of the old life.

Believers Are Children of Light

"For ye were sometimes darkness, but now are ye light in

the Lord: walk as children of light; (For the fruit of the Spirit is in all goodness and righteousness and truth;) Proving what is acceptable unto the Lord. And have no fellowship with the unfruitful works of darkness, but rather reprove them" (Eph. 5:8-11).

Here Paul gives the same exhortation that he gave to the Christians in Galatia. We are children of the light, for Jesus is the Light of the world, and we are in Him, He is in us. We are therefore not to grope in the darkness of this world. We are not to compromise with the things of the world, nor do the deeds of darkness from which no eternal good can ever come. We are commanded to "come out from among them, and be ye separate . . . and touch not the unclean [dark] thing" (II Cor. 6:17).

"Ye are the children of light, and the children of the day: we are not of the night, nor of darkness. Therefore let us not sleep, as do others; but let us watch and be sober. For they that sleep sleep in the night; and they that be drunken are drunken in the night. But let us, who are of the day, be sober, putting on the breastplate of faith and love; and for an helmet, the hope of salvation. For God hath not appointed us to wrath, but to obtain salvation by our Lord Jesus Christ" (I Thess. 5:5-9).

As children of God, bearing His name, we are not only to stand fast in the liberty wherewith Christ hath made us free, we are not only to walk in the light in paths of righteousness, led by the Holy Spirit, but we are also commanded to *watch and be sober*. The meaning here is that of a sentry on guard — one who must be alert every moment, who dares not sleep nor grow sluggish. A sentry who falls asleep on guard runs the risk of courtmartial. By comparison, Christians are children of the day, and we are to practice vigilance. We are never to be drowsy, spiritually speaking. We should be alert, on active duty, never deserting our post.

Jesus said, "What I say unto you, I say unto ALL: *Watch!*" (Mark 13:37). In John 14:2, 3, He promised, "I go to prepare a place for you. And if I go and prepare a place for you, *I will come again, and receive you unto myself*; that where I am,

there ye may be also!" He made the promise, HE WILL
RETURN.

At the ascension of Jesus, as the disciples gazed after Him
into the heavens, the heavenly messengers said to them, "Ye
men of Galilee, why stand ye gazing up into heaven? This
same Jesus, which is taken up from you into heaven, shall
so come in like manner as ye have seen Him go into heaven"
(Acts 1:10, 11).

Knowing that He WILL return as He promised, we should
never be caught off guard, we should never sleep on duty;
we should be alert at all times, we should "occupy until He
comes." The day of grace is sure to end. The day of the
Gospel opportunity has its limit, and one day this Gospel of
Grace will be preached no more. Therefore, Christians should
be active, alert, alive, busy in the service of the Lord so that
when He DOES come He will not come upon us unawares:

". . . Take heed to yourselves, lest at any time your hearts
be overcharged with surfeiting, and drunkenness, and cares
of this life, and so that day come upon you unawares" (Luke
21:34).

The multitudes of unbelievers are sleeping, walking in darkness, thoughtless, careless, unconcerned about their eternal
destiny. Apostate church members, like the five foolish virgins,
are slumbering. They are of the night. True believers,
children of the day, should always hear the echo of the words
of Jesus:

*"Watch therefore, for ye know neither the day nor the hour
wherein the Son of man cometh"* (Matt. 25:13).

Chapter VI

The Cross

The crucifixion of the Lord Jesus Christ is the greatest theme in all history. The message of the crucifixion proclaims the greatest, grandest work ever performed, by the greatest Person who ever lived; and through the work accomplished on the cross by the Lord Jesus Christ, the greatest blessing ever received by man is afforded.

The atonement of our Lord Jesus Christ is the heart, soul, and essence of the Word of God. The atonement is not a *part* of Christianity — it IS Christianity! In the atonement all human need is met, all human questions answered. In the atonement we find the balm for all human ills, anxieties, and fears, we find joy unspeakable and full of glory. In the atonement, *human guilt is removed.*

The preaching of the cross of the Lord Jesus Christ, the atoning sacrifice, is the only message that will convince men of sin. Peter preached this message on the Day of Pentecost:

"This Jesus hath God raised up, whereof we all are witnesses. Therefore being by the right hand of God exalted, and having received of the Father the promise of the Holy Ghost, He hath shed forth this, which ye now see and hear. For David is not ascended into the heavens: but he saith himself, The Lord said unto my Lord, Sit thou on my right hand, until I make thy foes thy footstool. *Therefore let all the house of Israel know assuredly, that God hath made that same Jesus, whom ye have crucified, both Lord and Christ*" (Acts 2:32-36).

The preaching of the atonement is the only message that will bring blessing to the poor, needy individual who is paralyzed by sin and bound by iniquity. In Acts 3:12-19, Peter again preached the message of the cross:

". . . Ye men of Israel, why marvel ye at this? or why look ye so earnestly on us, as though by our own power or holiness we had made this man to walk? The God of Abraham, and of Isaac, and of Jacob, the God of our fathers, hath glorified His Son Jesus; whom ye delivered up, and denied Him in the presence of Pilate, when he was determined to let Him go. But ye denied the Holy One and the Just, and desired a murderer to be granted unto you; and killed the Prince of life, whom God hath raised from the dead; whereof we are witnesses. And His name through faith in His name hath made this man strong, whom ye see and know: yea, the faith which is by Him hath given him this perfect soundness in the presence of you all. And now, brethren, I wot that through ignorance ye did it, as did also your rulers. But those things, which God before had shewed by the mouth of all His prophets, that Christ should suffer, He hath so fulfilled. Repent ye therefore, and be converted, that your sins may be blotted out, when the times of refreshing shall come from the presence of the Lord."

The preaching of the atonement is the only message that brings forgiveness. In Acts 5:29-31 Peter emphatically declared, ". . . We ought to obey God rather than men. The God of our fathers raised up Jesus, whom ye slew and hanged on a tree. Him hath God exalted with His right hand to be a Prince and a Saviour, for to give repentance to Israel, and forgiveness of sins."

The preaching of the atonement is the only message that will bring joy. It is the message that satisfied the heart of the Eunuch:

". . . The Spirit said unto Philip, Go near, and join thyself to this chariot. And Philip ran thither to him, and heard him read the prophet Esaias, and said, Understandest thou what thou readest? And (the eunuch) said, How can I, except some man should guide me? And he desired Philip that he would come up and sit with him. The place of the Scripture which he read was this, *He was led as a sheep to the slaughter; and like a lamb dumb before his shearer, so opened He not His mouth: In His humiliation His judgment was taken away: and who shall*

declare His generation? for His life is taken from the earth. And
the eunuch answered Philip, and said, I pray thee, of whom
speaketh the prophet this? of himself, or of some other man?
Then Philip opened his mouth, and began at the same Scripture,
and preached unto him Jesus. And as they went on their way,
they came unto a certain water: and the eunuch said, See, here
is water; what doth hinder me to be baptized? And Philip said,
If thou believest with all thine heart, thou mayest. And he answered and said, I believe that Jesus Christ is the Son of God.
And he commanded the chariot to stand still: and they went
down both into the water, both Philip and the eunuch; and he
baptized him. And when they were come up out of the water,
the Spirit of the Lord caught away Philip, that the eunuch saw
him no more: *and [the eunuch] went on his way rejoicing!"*
(Acts 8:29-39).

The preaching of the cross of the Lord Jesus Christ is the only
message that will bring the Holy Spirit to the heart. This is
made known in Peter's message to Cornelius in Acts 10:39-44:

"And we are witnesses of all things which He did both in the
land of the Jews, and in Jerusalem; whom they slew and hanged
on a tree: Him God raised up the third day, and shewed Him
openly; not to all the people, but unto witnesses chosen before
of God, even to us, who did eat and drink with Him after He
rose from the dead. And He commanded us to preach unto
the people, and to testify that it is He which was ordained of
God to be the Judge of quick and dead. To Him give all the
prophets witness, that through His name whosoever believeth
in Him shall receive remission of sins. *While Peter yet spake
these words, the Holy Ghost fell on all them which heard the
Word."*

The preaching of the cross and the shed blood is the only
medium of justification. Paul declared this truth at Antioch:

"Be it known unto you therefore, men and brethren, that
through this Man is preached unto you the forgiveness of sins:
And by Him all that believe are justified from all things, from
which ye could not be justified by the law of Moses" (Acts 13:
38, 39).

The reception of the message of the atonement imparts responsibility to the individual, especially to the ministers of Jesus Christ. Paul declared to the elders at Ephesus when he charged them to care for the purchased possession of Jesus, "Take heed therefore unto yourselves, and to all the flock, over the which the Holy Ghost hath made you overseers, to feed the Church of God, which He hath purchased with His own blood" (Acts 20:28).

To the Corinthians Paul declared, "For I determined not to know any thing among you, save Jesus Christ, and Him crucified. . . . That your faith should not stand in the wisdom of men, but in the power of God" (I Cor. 2:2, 5).

In I Corinthians 15:1-11 he declared, "Moreover, brethren, I declare unto you the Gospel which I preached unto you, which also ye have received, and wherein ye stand; by which also ye are saved, if ye keep in memory what I preached unto you, unless ye have believed in vain. For I delivered unto you first of all that which I also received, how that Christ died for our sins according to the Scriptures; and that He was buried, and that He rose again the third day according to the Scriptures: and that He was seen of Cephas, then of the twelve: After that, He was seen of above five hundred brethren at once; of whom the greater part remain unto this present, but some are fallen asleep. After that, He was seen of James; then of all the apostles. And last of all He was seen of me also, as of one born out of due time. For I am the least of the apostles, that am not meet to be called an apostle, because I persecuted the Church of God. But by the grace of God I am what I am: and His grace which was bestowed upon me was not in vain; but I laboured more abundantly than they all: yet not I, but the grace of God which was with me. Therefore whether it were I or they, so we preach, and so ye believed."

Writing to the believers in Galatia, Paul emphatically declared, ". . . God forbid that I should glory, save in the cross of our Lord Jesus Christ, by whom the world is crucified unto me, and I unto the world" (Gal. 6:14).

To the believers in Ephesus, his message was, "In whom we have redemption through His blood, the forgiveness of sins, according to the riches of His grace" (Eph. 1:7).

To the Colossians, "In whom we have redemption through His blood, even the forgiveness of sins" (Col. 1:14).

According to the Apostle Paul, the hub of the wheel of salvation is the cross of Jesus. All the spokes in the wheel connect to the hub — the atonement — and apart from the atonement there is no forgiveness, no remission, no redemption, no ransom paid, no new life. The atonement is the heart, soul, heartbeat, bloodstream, the very essence of salvation, from start to finish.

As He tabernacled among men, Jesus said, ". . . I thank thee, O Father, Lord of heaven and earth, because thou hast hid these things from the wise and prudent, and hast revealed them unto babes" (Matt. 11:25).

The Apostle Paul declares the same truth in different words in I Corinthians 2:14: "But the natural man receiveth not the things of the Spirit of God: for they are foolishness unto him: neither can he know them, because they are spiritually discerned."

What is the key that unlocks the Bible? What is the secret ingredient that causes one to love, appreciate, and understand the Word of God? It is not scholastic training, intellectual ability, or the wisdom of man. God is not found by searching. He is not found in a test tube in the laboratory. He is there, yes — but He is not *discovered* there by the seeker of truth. The only possible way to know the truth is to be willing to obey the living Word.

Jesus said to His disciples, "I have yet many things to say unto you, but ye cannot bear them now. Howbeit when He, the Spirit of truth, is come, He will guide you into all truth: for He shall not speak of Himself; but whatsoever He shall hear, that shall He speak; and He will shew you things to come. He shall glorify me: for He shall receive of mine, and shall shew it unto you" (John 16:12-14).

In the first epistle of John we read, "But ye have an unction from the Holy One, and ye know all things. I have not written unto you because ye know not the truth, but because ye know it, and that no lie is of the truth. . . . But the anointing which ye have received of Him abideth in you, and ye need not that any man teach you: but as the same anointing teacheth you of all things, and is truth, and is no lie, and even as it hath taught you, ye shall abide in Him. And now, little children, abide in Him;

that, when He shall appear, we may have confidence, and not be ashamed before Him at His coming" (I John 2:20-28 in part).

In I John 5:20 we read, "And we know that the Son of God is come, and hath given us an understanding, that we may know Him that is true, and we are in Him that is true, even in His Son Jesus Christ. This is the true God, and eternal life."

The message of the atonement is the center of every great doctrine of the Christian faith. These great doctrines are progressively revealed in the Scriptures. It was at Caesarea Philippi that the Lord Jesus first taught His disciples about the cross:

"From that time forth began Jesus to shew unto His disciples how that He must go unto Jerusalem, and suffer many things of the elders and chief priests and scribes, and be killed, and be raised again the third day. Then Peter took Him, and began to rebuke Him, saying, Be it far from thee, Lord: this shall not be unto thee. But [Jesus] turned and said unto Peter, Get thee behind me, Satan: thou art an offence unto me: for thou savourest not the things that be of God, but those that be of men. Then said Jesus unto His disciples, If any man will come after me, let him deny himself, and take up his cross, and follow me. For whosoever will save his life shall lose it: and whosoever will lose his life for my sake shall find it" (Matt. 16:21-25).

From that day forward, Jesus frequently spoke of His coming death and of what He must accomplish at Jerusalem. His death was a divine imperative.

The justice of God demanded it:

"Behold, all souls are mine; as the soul of the father, so also the soul of the son is mine: *the soul that sinneth, it shall die*" (Ezek. 18:4).

The holy law of God demanded the death of Jesus:

"Christ hath redeemed us from the curse of the law, being made a curse for us: for it is written, Cursed is every one that hangeth on a tree: That the blessing of Abraham might come on the Gentiles through Jesus Christ; that we might receive the promise of the Spirit through faith" (Gal. 3:13).

Man's sin called for the death of Jesus:

"Who was delivered for our offences, and was raised again for our justification" (Rom. 4:25).

The *wrath of God* is met in the death of Jesus:

"Much more then, being now justified by His blood, we shall be saved from wrath through Him" (Rom. 5:9).

The *holiness of God* is upheld by the death of Jesus:

"To declare, I say, at this time His righteousness: that He might be just, and the justifier of him which believeth in Jesus" (Rom. 3:26).

Mercy is obtained because of His death:

". . . Thus it is written, and thus it behooved Christ to suffer, and to rise from the dead the third day: And that repentance and remission of sins should be preached in His name among all nations, beginning at Jerusalem" (Luke 24:46, 47).

Divine wisdom and saving power are communicated to man through the atoning death of Jesus:

"But unto them which are called, both Jews and Greeks, Christ the power of God, and the wisdom of God" (I Cor. 1:24).

God the Father is glorified by the death of Jesus:

"Be ye therefore followers of God, as dear children; and walk in love, as Christ also hath loved us, and hath given Himself for us an offering and a sacrifice to God for a sweetsmelling savour" (Eph. 5:1, 2).

There are three passages in the New Testament in which Christ definitely refers to the divine necessity of His death:

1 – Through the baptism of His suffering.

2 – In the dying corn of wheat.

3 – In the uplifted Saviour.

He said:

"*I have a baptism to be baptized with;* and how am I straitened till it be accomplished!"(Luke 12:50).

"Verily, verily, I say unto you, *Except a corn of wheat fall into the ground and die, it abideth alone;* but if it die, it bringeth forth much fruit" (John 12:24). (Please note the word "*except.*" Here is pointed out a divine fact that a condition must be fulfilled before the end can be attained.)

". . . As Moses lifted up the serpent in the wilderness, *even so must the Son of man be lifted up*" (John 3:14).

The *baptism* mentioned points to the engulfing of the Saviour with all of the sorrow and heartache of all mankind, from Adam until the end.

The *dying corn of wheat* testifies that death is necessary to life.

The *uplifted Saviour* points to the cross upon which Jesus died.

The Lord Jesus Christ was the obedient, alert, and ardent servant of God the Father. He said, "I must be about my Father's business. . . . I must work the works of Him that sent me . . ." (Luke 2:49; John 9:4).

Christ came into the world with His eye singled on Calvary. He knew that He was born a king, *"but first must He suffer many things, and be rejected . . ."* (Luke 17:25). He was the Passover Lamb, and He knew that *"the Passover must be killed"* (Luke 22:7). He knew that the Scriptures must be fulfilled — the Old Testament prophecies of His Atonement: "For I say unto you, that *this that is written must yet be accomplished in me . . .* (Luke 22:37). He was the Crucified Christ: *"The Son of man must be delivered into the hands of sinful men, and be crucified . . ."* (Luke 24:7).

The Lord Jesus Christ was always ready to explain His mission. He said to the weary disciples on the road to Emmaus, "Ought not Christ to have suffered these things, and to enter into His glory? And beginning at Moses and all the prophets, He expounded unto them in all the Scriptures the things concerning Himself" (Luke 24:26, 27).

In the crucifixion of the Lord Jesus Christ, the Gospel is personified: ". . . Thus it is written, and thus it behooved Christ to suffer, and to rise from the dead the third day: and that repentance and remission of sins should be preached in His name among all nations, beginning at Jerusalem" (Luke 24:46, 47).

There is no doubt about it: If we believe the Word of God, if we receive it literally, *Christ had to come into the world and die on the cross.* If sinners were to be saved, there was no other way. There was no substitute, no other sacrifice. Christ was THE Lamb, THE Son, THE Atonement.

In Gethsemane Jesus prayed, "O my Father, *if it be possible,* let this cup pass from me! Nevertheless not as I will, but as thou

wilt" (Matt. 26:39). And since it was a divine impossibility for
the cup to pass, Christ drained it to the last bitter dregs and
went on to the death of the cross, so that He could say to the
heavenly Father, to the satisfaction of heaven and earth, to the
satisfaction of God's holiness, and to the defeat of death, hell, and
the grave, "IT IS FINISHED!!" (John 19:30).

The Gospels do not reveal the full truth concerning the cross
of Jesus, as proved by His words previously quoted from John
16:12, 13. He clearly taught His disciples that there were many
things that He had to say to them which they could not receive
or understand at that particular time. But He promised that the
Spirit of truth would come, and that when He came He would
guide them into ALL truth.

Not until the Day of Pentecost did the disciples recognize the
full significance of the cross of Jesus. Even *later* than Pentecost,
Paul was granted a special revelation when God called him,
anointed him, and commissioned him as the human instrument
to declare the way of justification of the sinner and the identification of the believer with Christ, in death and in resurrection.

First and foremost, the cross provides redemption. To the
sinner, the cross means salvation and forgiveness, and apart from
the cross there IS no salvation. Apart from the uplifted Saviour,
sinners could not come to God. Apart from the atonement, no
one could be saved. The Gospel is the power of God unto salvation unto every one that believeth — and the Gospel is the death,
burial, and resurrection of Jesus *"according to the Scriptures."*

The Meaning of the Cross to the Believer

The cross means salvation to the sinner, but this does not
mean the *end* of the cross in the life of the person who has become a Christian. Through the atonement, *he who believes* is
justified and adopted, but there is a still deeper truth in the message of the atonement — the truth of *identification*.

The fundamental truth wrapped up in identification is that
in the reckoning of God in His divine, eternal plan, the Lord
Jesus Christ not only died on the cross FOR us, but we who believe on Him *died IN HIM*. When one embraces the finished

work of Christ, that person becomes a recipient of all that Christ accomplished in the atonement.

Therefore, to the believer the cross includes sanctification as well as justification. The atonement deals with *sinfulness* as well as with *sin* — or shall we say that the cross in the life of the believer deals with *sins* (plural) as well as with SIN (singular) that damns the sinner (John 3:18).

Jesus came the first time to take away SIN: ". . . Behold the Lamb of God, which taketh away the SIN of the world" (John 1:29). NOW He ever lives as our Mediator, He is the propitiation for our SINS:

"For there is one God, and one Mediator between God and men, the man Christ Jesus" (I Tim. 2:5).

". . . And if any man sin, we have an Advocate with the Father, Jesus Christ the righteous: And He is the propitiation for our SINS: and not for our's only, but also for the sins of the whole world" (I John 2:1, 2).

Sanctification and justification rest upon the same foundation and proceed from the same source. There is but ONE foundation (I Cor. 3:11), *it is LAID*, Jesus Christ is the chief Cornerstone, and there can BE no other foundation.

For the believer, there are two aspects of the death of Christ: His death was, first, *for sin*, and He becomes our Redeemer when we are saved by trusting in His death, His shed blood. Then, in His crucifixion, His atonement, the believer *receives death UNTO sin*, which means that sin ceases to be the master of our lives. Sin no longer has dominion over us, for we are more than conquerors through Him that loved us. In His death, He not only robbed sin of its *penalty* — He also robbed sin of its *power*.

Christ's atonement not only separates the believer from the *consequences* of sin as transgression against God and His holy law; it also separates us from the *authority* of sin as master of our lives. Through the atonement, sin is no longer our master and we are no longer sin's slave. We can say with Paul, "I am crucified with Christ: nevertheless I live; yet not I, but Christ liveth in me . . ."

Our *identification with Christ* in His atonement does not have to do with the guilt from which we are delivered; it has to do with our *victory* over the world, the flesh, and the devil. This truth needs to be preached today as never before.

The "Old Man" Crucified

The Scriptures clearly teach that when we are born again, the "old man" is crucified:

"What shall we say then? Shall we continue in sin, that grace may abound? God forbid. How shall we that are *dead* to sin, live any longer therein? *Know ye not, that so many of us as were baptized into Jesus Christ were baptized into His death?* Therefore we are buried with Him by baptism into death: that like as Christ was raised up from the dead by the glory of the Father, even so we also should walk in newness of life.

"For if we have been planted together in the likeness of His death, we shall be also in the likeness of His resurrection: Knowing this, that *our old man is crucified with Him,* that the body of sin might be destroyed, that henceforth we should not serve sin. For he that is dead is freed from sin.

"Now if we be dead with Christ, we believe that we shall also live with Him: Knowing that Christ being raised from the dead dieth no more; death hath no more dominion over Him. For in that He died, He died unto sin once: but in that He liveth, He liveth unto God" (Rom. 6:1-10).

What IS *"the old man"*? He is our former inner self — what we were before we believed unto salvation. The "old man" is all that we were in our unregenerate state before the miracle of grace that placed us in the family of heaven. The "old man" is what we were as children of the first Adam. But when the unbeliever believes unto salvation, he becomes a NEW man, a new creation:

"Therefore if any man be in Christ, he is a new creature: old things are passed away; behold, all things are become new" (II Cor. 5:17).

In the Gospel according to Paul we are clearly taught that there are two distinct humanities, two human races on earth today — the *natural* man who sprang from the first Adam, and the *new* man who is the son of the last Adam:

"The first man is of the earth, earthy: the second Man is the
Lord from heaven. As is the earthy, such are they also that are
earthy; and as is the heavenly, such are they also that are heavenly. And as we have borne the image of the earthy, we shall
also bear the image of the heavenly" (I Cor. 15:47-49).

By generation (through the natural birth) we all belong to the
family of Adam, since he and Eve were the father and mother of
all living; but those of us who have believed and placed our trust
in the finished work of Jesus and His shed blood, by *regeneration*
belong to a new family — we are sons of God!

Jesus testified to His own people, the Jews, that He was the
light of the world, and tried to impress upon them the fact that
they could know the truth that would set them free; but they
argued with Him by saying that since Abraham was their father,
they had never been *in bondage.* He replied, "I know that ye
are Abraham's seed; but ye seek to kill me, because my Word
hath no place in you. . . . If ye were Abraham's children, ye
would do the works of Abraham. . . . *Ye are of your father
the devil, and the lusts of your father will ye do.* He was a murderer from the beginning, and abode not in the truth, because
there is no truth in him. When he speaketh a lie, he speaketh
of his own: for he is a liar, and the father of it. And because I
tell you the truth, ye believe me not" (John 8:12-45 in part).

Upon this earth today there are sons of God, and sons of Satan.
All born again believers are sons of God, all *unbelievers* are sons
of the devil whether they like to face that fact or not! Because
of sin, sons of Adam inherit the corrupt, Adamic nature. In
Adam, all die. Any unregenerate person has within his bosom a
nature capable of committing any horrible sin that any other person has ever committed. Let us look at a picture of the unregenerate heart:

". . . From within, out of the heart of men, proceed evil
thoughts, adulteries, fornications, murders, thefts, covetousness,
wickedness, deceit, lasciviousness, an evil eye, blasphemy, pride
foolishness: All these evil things come from within and defile
the man" (Mark 7:21-23).

"The heart is deceitful above all things, and desperately
wicked: who can know it?" (Jer. 17:9).

From the heart proceed the issues of life — and the heart of the unbeliever is sinful beyond imagination: but the believer has a NEW heart and a new life.

The Body of Sin

There is much controversy concerning *"the body of sin"* mentioned in Romans 6:6. Some teach that the statement means the sum of all indwelling sin — the sinful nature; but outstanding Bible scholars of the past have agreed that it means "the body belonging TO sin." It is an expression similar to "the shield of faith" or "the sword of the Spirit." The "shield of faith" does not mean the shield which is faith, but rather the shield which faith recognizes, grasps, and uses. The sword of the Spirit does not mean that the *Spirit* is the sword, but refers to the sword *which the Holy Spirit employs* to bring victory to the individual.

Thus, the "body of sin" does not mean the body which IS sin, but rather *the physical tabernacle which was claimed by sin as its very own* since in Adam we are *all* born in sin and shapen in iniquity. Sin has always reigned over and used the body of the natural man. The natural body has always been the tabernacle and stronghold of sin, the fort from which sin wages its battle to damn the soul.

We live in a body that is determined to damn us, we have within us a heart that is capable of manufacturing any sin known to man. The natural man is totally depraved, and therefore must be totally delivered from sin. Such deliverance is ours in the atonement.

The "old man" is crucified *"that the body of sin might be destroyed."* The Apostle Paul uses the word "destroyed" twenty-five times in his epistles, and out of the twenty-five times, it is translated seventeen different ways! The Greek word here rendered "destroyed" does not mean annihilation or total cessation. It means to be rendered powerless, or reduced to a state of inaction.

The teaching here is NOT that sin is *eradicated,* but that it is *robbed of its power.* There are those who teach that the old nature is completely eradicated when the sinner is saved, but facts prove the contrary — and those who teach such erroneous doctrine certainly have not proved it by the lives they live! As long as we remain in this earthly realm, we will possess the flesh (the Adamic nature) in that we will live the life of the natural man such as eating, association with our friends, and reproducing from the family standpoint. If the old nature were completely eradicated and changed into the spiritual, then the offspring of union between man and wife would of necessity be angelic or spiritual — and we know that such is not the case. Regardless of how spiritual, how dedicated, or how separated unto God a person may be, he still possesses the flesh, but the "old man" is reduced to a state of inaction.

If the old nature could be completely eradicated, there would have been no need for Paul to write to the Corinthians, *"Wherefore let him that thinketh he standeth take heed lest he fall.* There hath no temptation taken you but such as is common to man: but God is faithful, who will not suffer you to be tempted above that ye are able; but will with the temptation also make a way to escape, that ye may be able to bear it'* (I Cor. 10:12, 13).

The Scriptural Teaching Concerning the Crucifixion of the "Old Man"

In Romans 6:6 Paul clearly declares, "Our old man is crucified with Christ." In Colossians 3:9 he says, "Ye have put off the old man with his deeds." You will notice that Paul did not say, "The old man IS BEING crucified," nor that he "WILL BE crucified" at some future date. He did not say "You are *in the process* of putting off the old man," nor "The old man WILL BE put off at some future date." The tense of the verb shows it to be an accomplished fact. "The old man IS put off" (present tense). Paul's exhortation is for the believer to recognize the fact that, because we have died with Christ, the old man HAS BEEN put off.

Now, the admonition is to put off the *clothes* of the old man — *old habits* such as anger, malice, lying, abuse, slander, dishonesty, passion — anything that would fail to bring honor and glory to the Lord Jesus Christ. Paul is teaching that the "old man" has been crucified, put off, we are now new creations in

Christ Jesus, and IN HIM the "new man" is to follow in His steps and live as befits a child of God.

Here is exactly what happened on the cross: God made Christ to be sin for us (II Cor. 5:21). Thus, God, *in Christ,* identified Himself with sin, made Himself *identical with us IN our sin.* Now, the unbeliever — exercising faith in the atonement, believing in the finished work of Jesus Christ on the cross — by faith is *identified* with Christ in His death, burial, and resurrection. To be identified with one, according to the dictionary, is to "treat as *identical with.*" Therefore, we experience by faith all that Christ experienced in actuality FOR us on the cross!

When one of our loved ones dies, all human ties are broken, all fellowship and union with the departed one ceases. Since *we are dead with Christ,* hid with Christ in God (Col. 3:3), all fellowship and union with *sin* is broken off — and it happened at the cross! The sin-question has been settled — once, for all, forever. There is not one thing any person can do about the sin-debt. Jesus settled it *in full* in the atonement.

When the Lord Jesus Christ died on the cross, every believer died with Him:

"For the love of Christ constraineth us; because we thus judge, that if one died for all, then were all dead: And that He died for all, that they which live should not henceforth live unto themselves, but unto Him which died for them, and rose again. Wherefore henceforth know we no man after the flesh: yea, though we have known Christ after the flesh, yet now henceforth know we Him no more. Therefore if any man be in Christ, he is a new creature: old things are passed away; behold, all things are become new. And all things are of God, who hath reconciled us to Himself by Jesus Christ, and hath given to us the ministry of reconciliation: To wit, that God was in Christ, reconciling the world unto Himself, not imputing their trespasses unto them; and hath committed unto us the word of reconciliation. Now then we are ambassadors for Christ, as though God did beseech you by us: we pray you in Christ's stead, be ye reconciled to God. For He hath made Him to be sin for us, who knew no sin; that we might be made the righteousness of God in Him" (II Cor. 5:14-21).

"Husbands, love your wives, even as Christ also loved the Church, and gave Himself for it; that He might sanctify and cleanse it with the washing of water by the Word, that He might present it to Himself a glorious Church, not having spot, or wrinkle, or any such thing; but that it should be holy and without blemish" (Eph. 5:25-27).

Every born again person is a member of the New Testament Church, a member of Christ's body:

"For as the body is one, and hath many members, and all the members of that one body, being many, are one body: so also is Christ. For by one Spirit are we all baptized into one body, whether we be Jews or Gentiles, whether we be bond or free; and have been all made to drink into one Spirit. For the body is not one member, but many.

"If the foot shall say, Because I am not the hand, I am not of the body, is it therefore not of the body? And if the ear shall say, Because I am not the eye, I am not of the body, is it therefore not of the body? If the whole body were an eye, where were the hearing? If the whole were hearing, where were the smelling? But now hath God set the members every one of them in the body, as it hath pleased Him. And if they were all one member where the body? But now are they many members, yet but one body. And the eye cannot say unto the hand, I have no need of thee: nor again the head to the feet, I have no need of you. Nay, much more those members of the body, which seem to be more feeble, are necessary: and those members of the body, which we think to be less honourable, upon these we bestow more abundant honour; and our uncomely parts have more abundant comeliness.

"For our comely parts have no need: but God hath tempered the body together, having given more abundant honour to that part which lacked: That there should be no schism in the body; but that the members should have the same care one for another. And whether one member suffer, all the members suffer with it; or one member be honoured, all the members rejoice with it.

"Now are ye the body of Christ, and members in particular" (I Cor. 12:12-27).

We who are believers *look back* to the cross — and we can say that we were poor, unregenerate souls, *but in Christ we died on the cross.* We are crucified with Him; the old humanity was nailed to the cross when Jesus was nailed there. Since this is a divine fact, sin now has no right to our bodies, sin has no claim on us, sin has no authority to operate in our bodies. The power and dominion of sin have been crucified, sin's claim on the Christian has been destroyed. As members of the body of Christ, we are no longer slaves to sin and in bondage to iniquity.

Born again believers are united to the body of Christ through the miracle of the new birth. We have been given a new heart and a new spirit, the old man has been crucified. Therefore, Paul admonishes us, "Likewise reckon ye also yourselves to be dead indeed unto sin, but alive unto God through Jesus Christ our Lord. Let not sin therefore reign in your mortal body, that ye should obey it in the lusts thereof. Neither yield ye your members as instruments of unrighteousness unto sin: but yield yourselves unto God, as those that are alive from the dead, and your members as instruments of righteousness unto God. For sin shall not have dominion over you: for ye are not under the law, but under grace" (Rom. 6:11-14).

Christians are to reckon (consider) themselves dead unto sin. Therefore, when the tempter comes, we can say, "I cannot participate. *I am dead!* The man whom you once knew and controlled is no longer alive. I am a *new man,* and you have no claim on me, no authority over me. I am your slave no more!" Such reckoning and reasoning on the part of believers will work a miracle in their lives.

Those who drank drink no more — *because they are dead to drink.* Those who lived in lust and debauchery *no longer* live in lust and debauchery because they are dead to such things. Before I was saved, I committed various sins — I drank, I gambled, I cursed, I lied: but *the person I am NOW* never did those things! Oliver Greene *as he is today* did not exist until the day he was born again. My life, from the time of my natural birth to the moment I was saved, *is completely erased from the mind of God.* He has no record of my existence up to the moment when I was born again. Indeed, we are to reckon ourselves *dead unto sin, but alive unto God through Jesus Christ our Lord!*

In Romans 5:12-21 Paul speaks of two humanities — Adam's race, and the sons of Christ.

In Romans chapter 6 he contrasts two masters: *sin* (to which all unbelievers are slaves), and Christ.

In Romans 7:1-6 he illustrates spiritual truth under the figure of a woman having two husbands:

"Know ye not, brethren, (for I speak to them that know the law,) how that the law hath dominion over a man as long as he liveth? For the woman which hath an husband is bound by the law to her husband so long as he liveth; but if the husband be dead, she is loosed from the law of her husband. So then if, while her husband liveth, she be married to another man, she shall be called an adulteress: but if her husband be dead, she is free from that law; so that she is no adulteress, though she be married to another man.

"Wherefore, my brethren, ye also are become dead to the law by the body of Christ; that ye should be married to another, even to Him who is raised from the dead, that we should bring forth fruit unto God.

"For when we were in the flesh, the motions of sins, which were by the law, did work in our members to bring forth fruit unto death. But now we are delivered from the law, that being dead wherein we were held; that we should serve in newness of spirit, and not in the oldness of the letter."

Marriage is the highest form of union between two people on earth, and spiritual union between the believer and Christ is the highest union known to Almighty God. Jesus is the head and the foundation of the New Testament Church, He is the Bridegroom, the Saviour of the body — and He claims our hearts. We are His, we are members of His body:

"For we are members of His body, of His flesh, and of His bones" (Eph. 5:30). *Christ hath betrothed us to Himself forever!* He will never divorce us: ". . . I will betroth thee unto me for ever; yea, I will betroth thee unto me in righteousness, and in judgment, and in lovingkindness, and in mercies. I will even betroth thee unto me in faithfulness: and thou shalt know the Lord" (Hos. 2:19, 20).

Because HE lives, we live also. This is divine truth in the power of His resurrection — not merely because He LIVED, not because of his holy, perfect life, and not merely because He DIED; but *because He was RAISED,* we are enabled to walk in newness of life, testifying that we are more than conquerors through HIM.

The Works of the Flesh Crucified

Deeper and deeper we go into the tremendous truth contained in the cross of Jesus. Not only was the "old man" crucified with Christ, but the flesh (the self-life) was also crucified.

Paul uses three words to define the flesh: (1) Works; (2) lust; (3) affections.

"Now the works of the flesh are manifest, which are these: Adultery, fornication, uncleanness, lasciviousness, idolatry, witchcraft, hatred, variance, emulations, wrath, strife, seditions, heresies, envyings, murders, drunkenness, revellings and such like: of the which I tell you before, as I have also told you in time past, that they which do such things shall not inherit the kingdom of God" (Gal. 5:19-21).

Here Paul refers to the carnal appetite — the outburst of selfishness and self-indulgence — *all impurity.* All that we do should be done to the glory of God, not for the glory and comfort of self. The Pharisees asked Jesus, "What shall we do, that we might work *the works of God?*" He replied, "This is the work of God, THAT YE BELIEVE ON HIM WHOM (GOD) HATH SENT" (John 6:28, 29).

The Scriptures leave no doubt as to what the works of the *flesh* are — they are catalogued in detail in the verses just quoted from Galatians, and are in contrast with the fruit of the Spirit:

"But the fruit of the Spirit is love, joy, peace, longsuffering, gentleness, goodness, faith, meekness, temperance: against such there is no law" (Gal. 5:22, 23).

Only the *flesh* could crave evil thoughts and desires — the Holy Spirit would never have part in such thinking; and in

Galatians 5:24 Paul tells us, ". . . *They that are Christ's have crucified the flesh with the affections and lusts!*"

The Greek word here rendered "lust" can also be translated "passions." Thus the lusts of the flesh are unholy desires and inclinations that roam in our mind and take root in our heart. In Proverbs 4:23 we read, "Keep thy heart with all diligence; *for out of it are the issues of life!* Jesus said, "Whosoever looketh on a woman to lust after her hath committed adultery with her already *in his heart*" (Matt. 5:28). In Mark 7:21 Jesus said, ". . . *From within, out of the heart of men, proceed evil thoughts,* and in Proverbs 23:7 we read, "As he [any man] thinketh in his heart, *so is he!*"

The affections (emotions) of the flesh point to the entirety of our earthly makeup or nature, especially as having to do with rebellion against the Holy Spirit and the new nature received by regeneration. All born again persons possess two natures — the *new man,* and the tabernacle (this body of flesh) in which the new man dwells. We might catalogue the affections as "things displayed in everyday life," such as unkindness, impatience, irritability, jealousy, laziness, uncharitableness, pride, envy, vanity, worldly ambition, disloyalty, cowardice, slander. These characteristics give us a word picture of the flesh.

The Apostle Paul recognized the flesh as his greatest enemy; he hated it. He said, "I keep under [buffet] my body, and bring it into subjection: lest that by any means, when I have preached to others, I myself should be a castaway" (I Cor. 9:27). To "become a castaway" had nothing to do with Paul's salvation. It would have been for God to place him on the shelf and cease to use him to proclaim the good news of salvation through the Gospel of grace.

When Christ died on the cross in the atonement, this putrid, corrupting foul flesh was crucified *with* Him. All of the works, passions, and affections of the flesh were nailed to the cross of the Lamb of God. IN HIM we have escaped the bondage of sin. We are no longer slaves to iniquity, captives to the flesh. We are risen from the grave of sin, released from the penitentiary of iniquity. We are free indeed because "the Son hath made us free!"

To the Believer, the World is Crucified

Not only is the "old man" crucified, not only is the body of sin destroyed and the flesh crucified, but in the atonement the believer also experiences *the crucifixion of the world*:

"Grace be to you and peace from God the Father, and from our Lord Jesus Christ, *who gave Himself for our sins, that He might deliver us from this present evil world,* according to the will of God and our Father" (Gal. 1:4).

"God forbid that I should glory, save in the cross of our Lord Jesus Christ, by whom the world is crucified unto me, and I unto the world" (Gal. 6:14).

"Wherefore if ye be dead with Christ from the rudiments of the world, why, as though living in the world, are ye subject to ordinances, (Touch not; taste not; handle not; which all are to perish with the using;) after the commandments and doctrines of men?" (Col. 2:20-22).

In the Scriptures, the Greek word translated "world" is used in three ways:

The *physical world,* the world of matter — mountains, fields, trees. "The earth is the Lord's, and the fulness thereof; the world, and they that dwell therein" (Psalm 24:1).

The racial world, its population — the human race which God so loved: "For God so loved the world, that He gave His only begotten Son, that whosoever believeth in Him should not perish, but have everlasting life" (John 3:16).

The "evil world" — the materialistic, humanistic systems and secular things. It is in this connection that Satan is declared to be the prince of the power of the air, and the god of this world:

"But if our Gospel be hid, it is hid to them that are lost: in whom *the god of this world* hath blinded the minds of them which believe not, lest the light of the glorious Gospel of Christ, who is the image of God, should shine unto them" (II Cor. 4:3, 4).

"And you hath He quickened, who were dead in trespasses and sins: Wherein in time past ye walked according to the course of this world, according to *the prince of the power of the*

air, the spirit that now worketh in the children of disobedience"
(Eph. 2:1, 2).

John the Beloved tells us that *"the whole world* lieth in
wickedness" (or, "in the lap of the wicked one"). The "world"
consists of places, persons, pleasures — and anything else — that
is against God and righteousness. Christians are crucified to the
world, the world is crucified to us — and the believer should
have the same fellowship with the world that two corpses have
as they rest beside each other in a morgue! That is exactly
the meaning of Galatians 6:14.

"Christ hath redeemed us from the curse of the law, being
made a curse for us: for it is written, Cursed is every one that
hangeth on a tree" (Gal. 3:13). Crucifixion was the most igno-
minious, shameful, debased form of execution known to man.
Thus, to be crucified to the world means that in the sight of the
world the believer is an enemy, hated and despised. For the
world to be crucified to the believer simply means that the
world has become an object of hatred to the Christian. This
is borne out in I John 2:15-17:

"Love not the world, neither the things that are in the world.
If any man love the world, the love of the Father is not in him.
For all that is in the world, the lust of the flesh, and the lust of
the eyes, and the pride of life, is not of the Father, but is of
the world. And the world passeth away, and the lust thereof:
but he that doeth the will of God abideth for ever."

The world is crucified to the believer, the believer is crucified
to the world. Thus we have a *double crucifixion,* a mutual hatred
one toward the other. The world no longer holds any attraction
for the believer, and the believer is certainly unwelcome in the
world! The born again child of God feeds on the milk, meat,
bread, and living water of the Word, while the world feeds on
darkness, lasciviousness, evil of all kinds.

The Christian looks at the world only to hate and abhor its
practices, because it was the sin of the human family and the
systems of the world that nailed the Lord Jesus to the cross.
Since the world is responsible for the crucifixion of my Lord, the
world assuredly holds no charm for me!

Sad to say, the tragedy of this hour is that we look at the

church — and we see the *world*. We look in the world — and see the *church!* There is entirely too much in common between the world and the church — (and when I say "the church," I am speaking of the *visible* church, the local assembly; not the true Church in which there is no spot or wrinkle).

The Christian should not find pleasure, satisfaction, or glory in the world. As new creations in Christ Jesus we should "seek those things which are above, where Christ sitteth on the right hand of God." We should set our affection on things above, not on things on the earth, for we are dead, and our lives are hid with Christ in God" (Col. 3:1-3).

How Can This Be True in the Christian's Life?

There is but one answer to this question, and that answer is found in the Word of God:

"Likewise reckon ye also yourselves to be dead indeed unto sin, but alive unto God through Jesus Christ our Lord" (Rom. 6:11).

We know that Christ died on the cross, we know that He died to pay the penalty for sin, to deliver us from the power of sin and make possible our fellowship with Himself. In I John 1:3, 4 we read, "That which we have seen and heard declare we unto you, *that ye also may have fellowship with us: and truly our fellowship is with the Father, and with His Son Jesus Christ. And these things write we unto you, that your joy may be full."*

Every Christian should read, re-read, and *memorize* the first epistle of John. It is the spiritual birthright of every believer to enjoy FULL JOY — but this can never be true in a life until that individual believer reckons himself dead unto sin, and then reckons himself alive unto God!

Does It Really Work?

Someone may be asking, "Does this really work in daily living?" Yes, it does! When temptation comes, when the world offers us the things of the old life which we once loved and practiced, we are to reckon ourselves dead, crucified with Christ, and then reckon ourselves a new creation ALIVE UNTO GOD. Christ lives in me — and since He is watching every move and knows every thought and intent of my heart, I must reckon myself dead to the world, but *living* in Jesus!

True, living faith is simply to KNOW that when Christ died on the cross, we died with Him; and when Christ rose again, we *rose* with Him. When Christ ascended, we ascended with Him, and *positionally* we are now seated with Christ Jesus in the heavenlies (Eph. 2:6, 7).

These are definite, positive, Bible facts. Reckon on them, and you will find that they work a miracle in your spiritual life! As a born again believer you are a corpse to the world — the "old man" is dead. To the believers in Rome, Paul said:

"I beseech you therefore, brethren, by the mercies of God, that ye present your bodies *a living sacrifice*, holy, acceptable unto God, which is your reasonable service, and be not conformed to this world; but be ye transformed by the renewing of your mind, that ye may prove what is that good, and acceptable, and perfect, will of God" (Rom. 12:1, 2).

"Neither yield ye your members as instruments of unrighteousness unto sin: but yield yourselves unto God, as those that are alive from the dead, and your members as instruments of righteousness unto God" (Rom. 6:13).

If, like Abraham, we are willing to *believe God,* if we are willing to take Him at His word and yield body and soul unreservedly into His hands, He will lead us in the path of righteousness; and regardless of what the devil may hurl across our pathway, God will make a way of escape for us!

God furnishes the armor and the weapons for the battle we must fight:

"Finally, my brethren, be strong in the Lord, and in the power of His might. Put on the whole armour of God, that ye may be able to stand against the wiles of the devil. For we wrestle not against flesh and blood, but against principalities, against powers, against the rulers of the darkness of this world, against spiritual wickedness in high places. Wherefore take unto you the whole armour of God, that ye may be able to withstand in the evil day, and having done all, to stand. Stand therefore, having your loins girt about with truth, and having on the breastplate of righteousness; and your feet shod with the preparation of the Gospel of peace; above all, taking the shield of faith, wherewith ye shall be able to quench all the fiery darts of the wicked. And take the helmet of salvation, and the sword of the Spirit, which is the Word of God: Praying always with all prayer and supplication in the Spirit, and watching thereunto with all perseverance and supplication for all saints" (Eph. 6:10-18).

Paul warned Timothy, "But thou, O man of God, flee these things; and follow after righteousness, godliness, faith, love, patience, meekness. Fight the good fight of faith, lay hold on eternal life, whereunto thou art also called, and hast professed a good profession before many witnesses" (I Tim. 6:11, 12).

A teacher or minister advertises Bible ignorance when he presents the Christian life as an *easy* life, a pathway strewn with flowers. In the epistles we are declared to be soldiers in a battle, runners in a race, servants who are not our own but bought with a price, and we are commanded to yield everything to God.

The Scriptures clearly declare, "Yea, and all that will live godly in Christ Jesus shall suffer persecution" (II Tim. 3:12).

Jesus Himself warned, ". . . *In the world ye shall have tribulation*: but be of good cheer; I have overcome the world" (John 16:33).

Peter admonished, *"Beloved, think it not strange concerning the fiery trial which is to try you,* as though some strange thing happened unto you: But rejoice, inasmuch as ye are partakers of Christ's sufferings; that, when His glory shall be revealed, ye may be glad also with exceeding joy" (I Pet. 4:12, 13).

There is no question about it: *Godly people suffer persecution.* But when we read in the Gospels what the Lord Jesus suffered for US, we dare not do less than take up the cross and follow Him daily.

Paul reminds the Hebrew believers, "Ye have not yet resisted unto blood, striving against sin" (Heb. 12:4).

This is no ordinary battle in which we are engaged! This battle is ugly and hot. The darts of the devil and the bullets of the damned are thick and plentiful. But we know who the Victor is, and we are more than conquerors through Him.

In Revelation 12:7-12 we find these comforting words:

"There was war in heaven: Michael and his angels fought against the dragon; and the dragon fought and his angels, *and prevailed not*; neither was their place found any more in heaven. And the great dragon was cast out, that old serpent, called the Devil, and Satan, which deceiveth the whole world: he was cast out into the earth, and his angels were cast out with him. And I heard a loud voice saying in heaven, Now is come salvation, and strength, and the kingdom of our God, and the power of His Christ: for the accuser of our brethren is cast down, which accused them before our God day and night. AND THEY OVERCAME HIM BY THE BLOOD OF THE LAMB, and by the word of their testimony; and they loved not their lives unto the death. Therefore rejoice, ye heavens, and ye that dwell in them. Woe to the inhabiters of the earth and of the sea! for the devil is come down unto you, having great wrath, *because he knoweth that he hath BUT A SHORT TIME!*"

Chapter VII

Sanctification

We have studied *justification*, which has to do with our standing and position as believers before God — we are justified *by faith.*

We have studied *adoption*, which has to do with our position in relation to God as His children — heirs of God, joint-heirs with Christ.

We have studied *identification* — the deeper meaning of the cross in identifying ourselves with the Father in the death, burial, and resurrection of the Lord Jesus Christ.

Now we go a little deeper into spiritual truths and learn that Christ is made unto us . . . *sanctification*:

". . . Base things of the world, and things which are despised, hath God chosen, yea, and things which are not, to bring to nought things that are: that no flesh should glory in His presence. But of Him are ye in Christ Jesus, *who of God is made unto us wisdom, and righteousness, and SANCTIFICA-TION, and redemption*: That, according as it is written, *He that glorieth, let him glory in the Lord*" (I Cor. 1:28-31).

"Sanctify them through thy truth: THY WORD is truth" (John 17:17).

Many dear people — even believers — think that justification, regeneration, adoption, sanctification, and redemption are all one and the same. It is true that they all have to do with our complete salvation in Christ, *but they are not synonymous*:

Justification concerns our position IN Christ; *regeneration* has to do with our condition *through* Christ after we are justified; *adoption* has to do with our status as children of God; but *sanctification* has to do with our progress as we grow into full maturity in the family of God. Sanctification reveals to us the deeper meaning of the Holy Spirit in our lives.

Even a babe in Christ *possesses* the Holy Spirit, but the Spirit continues to work in the life of that babe in Christ until he becomes mature and full grown, spiritually speaking. Sanctification teaches that the Holy Spirit not only *regenerates* us (thus imparting divine nature), but that day by day He transforms us into the likeness of Christ.

Regeneration, justification, adoption, and identification all emphasize the blessings of Calvary. *Sanctification* will reveal to us the blessing of Pentecost.

All Believers Are Sanctified

All born again believers are sanctified positionally; this occurs simultaneously with the new birth. To sanctify is to *set apart,* and the moment we are saved, we are translated out of the family of the devil into the family of God, out of the kingdom of darkness into the kingdom of light. Thus, all born again believers are sanctified *positionally*; but *experimentally* we are sanctified daily as we grow in grace.

To the Thessalonian Christians Paul said, ". . . God hath from the beginning chosen you to salvation *through sanctification of the Spirit and belief of the truth*" (II Thess. 2:13). In the Old Testament era, even animals, fields, and houses were sanctified, set apart for God. Study Leviticus 27:14-34.

The word "sanctification" in Old Testament times did not generally refer to an *inward* change, but that the material things as well as *people* were set apart for God to be used of Him.

But the New Testament meaning of sanctification suggests an inward work, cleansing from defilement, transforming the believer into holiness. As used in I Peter 3:15, it means to make holy by cleansing from sin:

". . . Sanctify the Lord God in your hearts: and be ready always to give an answer to every man that asketh you a reason of the hope that is in you with meekness and fear."

We do not grow INTO grace, but we do grow IN grace after we are the recipients of grace, having been born again. We do not grow into possession of the Holy Spirit, but we should be enlarged in the inner man as we grow in grace. We should be *filled* with the Spirit.

It Is God's Will That Believers Be Sanctified

Writing to the believers in Thessalonica, Paul said, ". . . This is the will of God, even your sanctification . . ." (I Thess. 4:3). Paul had a burden, not only to see people saved, but that his converts grow in grace and become stronger in the Lord. He rebuked the believers in Corinth because they were "carnal, even as unto babes in Christ, "and must be fed with milk instead of with meat. God wants for His children what any sincere parent wants for an earthly child. It is heartbreaking for parents to see their child stunted, sickly, failing to grow and become strong.

It is not God's will that we remain babes in Christ. Although we are instructed to manifest the spirit of a child in humility, forgiveness, and trust, we are to grow into *spiritual maturity*. In His Sermon on the Mount Jesus said, "Be ye therefore perfect, as your Father which is in heaven is perfect" (Matt. 5:48). This has nothing to do with sinlessness in the same sense that *Jesus* was sinless. It refers to maturity.

In Romans 8:28, 29 Paul said, ". . . We know that all things work together for good to them that love God, to them who are called according to His purpose. *For whom He did foreknow He also did predestinate to be conformed to the image of His Son . . .*"

In Ephesians 1:3-5 we read, "Blessed be the God and Father of our Lord Jesus Christ, who hath blessed us with all spiritual blessings in heavenly places in Christ: according as He hath chosen us in Him before the foundation of the world, *that we should be holy and without blame before Him in love*: Having predestinated us unto the adoption of children by Jesus Christ to Himself, according to the good pleasure of His will."

Greek scholars tell us that the Greek word here translated "predestinate" points to the ultimate goal of God's purpose for the believer. From the eternity behind us, God looked down through the ages; and in the mystery of His sovereign, divine will and wisdom, He saw (foreknew) those in every corner of the whole world who, from the creation of Adam to the last individual on the face of the earth, would respond to the Gospel call!

This foreknowledge of God has not one thing to do with the free will of man. Since God is sovereign and knows all things, *it was impossible for Him NOT to know* those who would believe — but this does not determine WHO WILL believe. It is up to the individual to accept or reject the Gospel.

God even gave Cain a second chance, but he turned it down. (Read Genesis 4:1-7.) To His own people Jesus said, *"Ye will not come to me,* that ye might have life" (John 5:40). As He wept over Jerusalem, He sorrowfully said, "O Jerusalem, Jerusalem, thou that killest the prophets, and stonest them which are sent unto thee, how often would I have gathered thy children together, even as a hen gathereth her chickens under her wings, AND YE WOULD NOT!" (Matt. 23:37).

Yes, man's will is free to accept or reject salvation — but God foreknew (foresaw) all who *would believe,* and for each of them He purposed and predestined that they should be conformed to the image of His Christ. And one glorious day the Church WILL be presented — without spot, wrinkle, or any such thing. Each and every member of that body will be perfect, without flaw! Therefore, Paul reminds us again and again that sanctification is the desire and the expressly determined will of God the Father for each child of His.

There is no such thing as a partial work of grace. Every believer has been saved from the guilt and penalty of sin. The very moment we believe on the Lord Jesus Christ and trust in His shed blood we are born into the family of God — just as redeemed as we will *ever* be. Redemption is past tense — we were redeemed the moment we put our faith in Jesus, redeemed from the *penalty* of sin. But we are being saved day by day from the *power* of sin.

Jesus ever lives to make intercession for us. He does not want us to sin, but if we DO sin we have an Advocate with the Father, Jesus Christ our Lord who is the propitiation for our sins. (Study I John 1:8-10; 2:1, 2.)

In the by-and-by God will save us from the very *presence* of sin — it may be today, it could be this very hour! We will be caught up in the clouds to meet Jesus in the air, lifted above this realm of sin. We will be caught out of this present evil world, and we will look on sin no more. God has predestined this for every child of His.

Redemption, justification, and adoption are instantaneous. *Sanctification* (positionally) is instantaneous, but *experimentally* it is a continued process of the working of the Holy Spirit within us until we see Jesus face to face. Then *we shall be like Him*: "Beloved, now are we the sons of God, and it doth not yet appear what we shall be: but we know that, when He shall appear, we shall be like Him; for we shall see Him as He is" (I John 2:2).

Because "the disciples were called Christians first in Antioch" (Acts 11:26), there are those who say the name "Christian" is a nickname, a name given in derision — *but not so!* A Christian is not an *imitation* of Christ — he is a *reproduction* of Christ. *Every believer is Christ reincarnated.*

For example, Jesus said to the Greeks, "Except a corn of wheat fall into the ground and die, it abideth alone: but if it die, it bringeth forth much fruit" (John 12:24). While Jesus was in a body, present with His disciples here on earth, His services and blessings to mankind were limited. But He changed His presence for *omnipresence*, and though He does not walk upon the earth now, He dwells in the heart of every true believer the world over, in the Person of the Holy Spirit!

The Results

To the Galatians Paul said, "Walk in the Spirit, and ye shall not fulfil the lust of the flesh" (Gal. 5:16). When one is born again, the old nature is not eradicated — it is *counteracted*. It ceases to function, but as long as we live in a body of flesh, we will have the *nature of the flesh.*

In Galatians 5:17 Paul said, ". . . *The flesh lusteth against the Spirit, and the Spirit against the flesh: and these are contrary the one to the other; so that ye cannot do the things that ye would.*" It is evident that Paul did not believe in eradication of the old nature. He taught that if we *walk in the Spirit,* we will not *fulfil* the lust of the flesh, but the flesh is there, and WILL BE there until we depart this life and receive our glorified body. Sanctification is not "a second work of grace" whereby the old nature (the flesh) is done away with (eradicated); but when we possess the Holy Spirit we possess a power within that brings about counteraction.

In Romans 8:1, 2 we read, "There is therefore now no condemnation to them which are in Christ Jesus, who walk not after the flesh, but after the Spirit. For the law of the Spirit of life in Christ Jesus hath made me free from the law of sin and death."

You will notice that this passage is positive. The statement is not "IF we walk not after the flesh." Believers "walk NOT" after the flesh — and the reason they walk not after the flesh is because the Lord is the Shepherd of the Christian, and the Shepherd leads into paths of right living.

The same truth is plainly declared in I John 5:4: ". . . Whatsoever [whosoever] is born of God overcometh the world: and this is the victory that overcometh the world, even our faith." This, too, is a positive statement. *Whosoever is born of God overcomes the world,* and the victory is faith.

The reason we overcome is clearly stated in I John 4:4: "Ye are of God, little children, and have overcome them: *because greater is He that is in you, than he that is in the world.*" The Holy Spirit is greater than the spirit of the devil. Jesus is greater than the devil himself. Therefore, believers are overcomers — there is no "maybe so, hope so, or perhaps" about it.

But notice: The Christian does not have victory *because the old nature has been removed.* He has victory because there is *Someone within him* who is greater than anyone without. The believer possesses the Holy Spirit in his heart, and there is NO heart big enough to contain both the Spirit of God and the spirit of Satan! Thus, Satan must tempt the believer from without, and when temptation comes, since the Lord Jesus Christ dwells in our hearts in the Person of the Holy Spirit, the devil will flee from us when we resist him.

Through the presence of the Holy Spirit, Christ reproduces himself in our lives; and what we cannot eradicate as long as we are in this body of flesh, the Holy Spirit can neutralize by His mighty counteracting power. Even though God does not *remove* the old nature, the Holy Spirit renders it inactive and unproductive. God does not place the believer in a position where it is utterly impossible for him to sin, but the grace of God makes provision for the Christian who does stumble. God has given us the Holy Spirit, to lead us, to direct us, to seal us, and to mold us day by day into the image of His dear Son.

What Is the Process of Progressive Sanctification?

We are saved by God's grace through faith — and there is only one way to obtain saving faith: *"So then faith cometh by hearing and hearing by the Word of God"* (Rom. 10:17).

Jesus said, "Verily, verily, I say unto you, *He that heareth my Word, and believeth on Him that sent me,* hath everlasting life, and shall not come into condemnation; but is passed from death unto life" (John 5:24).

Peter said, "Being born again, not of corruptible seed, but of incorruptible, *by the Word of God,* which liveth and abideth for ever" (I Pet. 1:23).

James said, "Wherefore lay apart all filthiness and superfluity of naughtiness, and receive with meekness *the engrafted Word,* which is able to save your souls" (James 1:21).

In Romans 1:16, 17 Paul said, ". . . I am not ashamed of the Gospel of Christ: *for it is the power of God unto salvation to every one that believeth*; to the Jew first, and also to the Greek. For therein is the righteousness of God revealed from faith to faith: as it is written, *The just shall live by faith!"*

The Scriptures make it clear that salvation comes only by hearing the Word, and the same is true of sanctification. We are sanctified through the Word (John 17:17). Jesus said to His disciples, "Now ye are *clean* through the WORD which I have spoken unto you" (John 15:3).

We are sanctified *progressively* as we feed upon the living Word. The Word is milk, meat, and bread whereby we grow. "The Word of God is quick, and powerful, and sharper than any twoedged sword, piercing even to the dividing asunder of soul and spirit, and of the joints and marrow, and is a discerner of the thoughts and intents of the heart" (Heb. 4:12). Any dead limbs in the Christian's life that need to be pruned off, the sword of the Spirit will cut them away.

The Spirit not only uses the pruning knife — but He also shows us the dead, unproductive limbs that need to be cut away. Of the Holy Spirit, Jesus promised, ". . . He shall take of mine, and shall shew it unto you" (John 16:15). As mentioned earlier in the message, the Holy Spirit did not come into the world for the purpose of empowering believers, nor just to lead the believer nor to seal us until the day of redemption — nor even to *fill* believers. The Holy Spirit is in the world to exalt, honor, and glorify Christ, and to make Him known to us in all of His glorious beauty and riches in grace!

We cannot gaze upon the glory and beauty of Christ without being aware of our own shortcomings and failures. When we look into the mirror of God's Word, and the Holy Spirit takes of the things of God and shows them unto us, we will see how far we come short of God's glory, and strive to be more like the Master.

> More like the Master I would ever be,
> More of His meekness, more humility;
> More zeal to labor, more courage to be true,
> More consecration for work He bids me do.
>
> More like the Master is my daily prayer;
> More strength to carry crosses I must bear;
> More earnest effort to bring His kingdom in;
> More of His spirit, the wanderer to win.
>
> More like the Master I would live and grow;
> More of His love to others I would show;
> More self-denial, like His in Galilee,
> More like the Master I long to ever be.
>
> Take Thou my heart, I would be Thine alone;
> Take Thou my heart and make it all Thine own;
> Purge me from sin, O Lord, I now implore,
> Wash me and keep me, Thine forever more!

One phase of the work of the Holy Spirit in the life of the believer is to convict him of the *sins of omission*. It is not always what the Christian *does* that robs him of power. More often, it is the sin of *omission* that robs him. The Holy Spirit reveals the things that are wrong in our lives — and then gives us courage and grace to make them right. He will show us the things that are lacking, and reveal to us how we can receive these things:

"But we all, with open face beholding as in a glass the glory of the Lord, are changed into the same image from glory to glory, even as by the Spirit of the Lord" (II Cor. 3:18).

For the Ephesians, Paul prayed "that [God] would grant you, according to the riches of His glory, to be strengthened with might by His Spirit in the inner man; that Christ may dwell in your hearts by faith; that ye, being rooted and grounded in love, may be able to comprehend with all saints what is the breadth, and length, and depth, and height; and to know the love of Christ, which passeth knowledge, that ye might be filled with all the fulness of God (Eph. 3:16-19).

Paul prayed the same prayer in other words for the Christians at Colosse:

"For this cause we also, since the day we heard it, do not cease to pray for you, and to desire that ye might be filled with the knowledge of His will in all wisdom and spiritual understanding; that ye might walk worthy of the Lord unto all pleasing, being fruitful in every good work, and increasing in the knowledge of God: Strengthened with all might, according to His glorious power, unto all patience and longsuffering with joyfulness" (Col. 1:9-11).

Fellow believer, did you know that all of God's resources, all of God's power, and the fulness of His grace, are at our disposal — *IN Christ, indwelt by the Holy Spirit?* The Apostle Paul declared, ". . . I take pleasure in infirmities, in reproaches, in necessities, in persecutions, in distresses for Christ's sake: for when I am weak, then am I strong!" (II Cor. 12:10).

The Holy Spirit convicts us of sin, draws us to God, "borns" us into the kingdom of God, indwells us, teaches us, assures us, leads us, and seals us "until the day of redemption" — but He does more:

". . . Be not drunk with wine, wherein is excess; but *be filled* with the Spirit; speaking to yourselves in psalms and hymns and spiritual songs, singing and making melody in your heart to the Lord; giving thanks always for all things unto God and the Father in the name of our Lord Jesus Christ" (Eph. 5:18-20).

The Christian may rest assured that being filled with the Spirit is the perfect antidote for every temptation hell can hurl at him. As we feed upon the Word of God, as we are led by the Spirit to walk in the light, the desire for things of the flesh leaves us. This is the result of *progressive sanctification*. We find here the living proof of II Corinthians 5:17: *"Therefore if any man be in Christ, he is a new creature: old things are passed away; behold, all things are become new."* We find that the things we once loved, we now hate; and the things we once hated; we now love. This is possible in the life of a Spirit-filled believer.

The Holy Spirit not only puts divine nature within us, but through progressive sanctification He transforms us:

"I beseech you therefore, brethren, by the mercies of God, that ye present your bodies a living sacrifice, holy, acceptable unto God, which is your reasonable service. And be not conformed to this world: but be ye *transformed by the renewing of your mind*, that ye may prove what is that good, and acceptable, and perfect, will of God" (Rom. 12:1, 2).

"Not by works of righteousness which we have done, but according to His mercy He saved us, *by the washing of regeneration, and renewing of the Holy Ghost*" (Tit. 3:5).

Scholars tell us that the Greek word here translated "transform" is the same word used in the account of the transfiguration in Matthew 17, where our Lord was "transfigured." As we grow older in the Lord, we are no more *saved* than we were at the time of the new birth, but we do grow more like the Christ with whom we walk and fellowship. The experience of every born again believer should be:

Every day with Jesus is sweeter than the day before.
Every day with Jesus, I love Him more and more.
Jesus saves and keeps me, and He's the One I'm living for.
Every day with Jesus is sweeter than the day before!

Do We Have Any Part in Progressive Sanctification?

There are certain things that the Christian cannot do for himself, and these things God will joyfully, willingly, do. There are other things that the believer CAN do, and God expects him to do those things for himself. For instance, we can "come out from among them," and be separate, and touch not the unclean thing (II Cor. 6:17). We can "present our bodies" in living sacrifice (Rom. 12:1). We can obey Hebrews 12:1:

"Wherefore seeing we also are compassed about with so great a cloud of witnesses, let us lay aside every weight, and the sin which doth so easily beset us, and let us run with patience the race that is set before us."

We can obey the instructions of Ephesians 5:7-17:

"Be not ye therefore partakers with them. For ye were sometimes darkness, but now are ye light in the Lord: walk as children of light: (For the fruit of the Spirit is in all goodness and righteousness and truth;) Proving what is acceptable unto the Lord. And have no fellowship with the unfruitful works of darkness, but rather reprove them. For it is a shame even to speak of those things which are done of them in secret. But all things that are reproved are made manifest by the light: for whatsoever doth make manifest is light. Wherefore He saith, Awake thou that sleepest, and arise from the dead, and Christ shall give thee light. *See then ye walk circumspectly, not as fools, but as wise, redeeming the time, because the days are evil. Wherefore be ye not unwise, but understanding what the will of the Lord is!*"

We can refuse to take part in anything that is questionable. We can prove all things and follow that which is good. We can be alert, wise in all of our daily practices of life. We can walk circumspectly, redeeming the time, for there is much that we can do — and that which we cannot do, God will happily do FOR us!

"Having therefore these promises, dearly beloved, let us cleanse ourselves from all filthiness of the flesh and spirit, perfecting holiness in the fear of God" (II Cor. 7:1).

Centuries ago, Jehovah thundered out, "I AM THE LORD

YOUR GOD! Ye shall therefore sanctify yourselves, and ye shall be holy; for I am holy: Neither shall ye defile yourselves with any manner of creeping thing that creepeth upon the earth" (Lev. 11:44).

God the Father calls upon His children to be willing to separate themselves from all that is evil, unrighteous, and un-Christlike. In I Thessalonians 5:16-24 Paul commanded:

"Rejoice evermore. Pray without ceasing. In every thing give thanks: for this is the will of God in Christ Jesus concerning you. Quench not the Spirit. Despise not prophesyings. Prove all things; hold fast that which is good. Abstain from all appearance of evil. And the very God of peace sanctify you wholly; and I pray God your whole spirit and soul and body be preserved blameless unto the coming of our Lord Jesus Christ. *Faithful is He that calleth you, who also will do it.*"

Believers are IN the world, but not OF the world. In His intercessory prayer, the Saviour besought the heavenly Father on our behalf: "I pray not that thou shouldest take them out of the world, but that thou shouldest keep them from the evil. They are not of the world, even as I am not of the world" (John 17:15, 16).

We are pilgrims on a journey. We seek those things which are above, where Christ sits on the right hand of God the Father. We are soldiers in the army of the Lord and we should sever relations with all things of this world that would hinder us as good soldiers of Jesus Christ:

"*No man that warreth entangleth himself with the affairs of this life*; that he may please Him who hath chosen him to be a soldier" (II Tim. 2:4).

We cannot avoid rubbing shoulders with the world, we cannot avoid coming in contact with evil; but we can — and we *must* — deliberately renounce evil and refuse to become involved in anything that would bring reproach upon the name of Christ.

"Whether therefore ye eat, or drink, or whatsoever ye do, do all to the glory of God" (I Cor. 10:31).

"For all things are yours . . . and ye are Christ's; and Christ is God's" (I Cor. 3:21, 23).

Chapter VIII

The Believer and the World

The question has been asked by many sincere believers, "What should be the feeling and attitude of a Christian toward the world — its habits, its ambitions, its pastimes and pleasures — and how should a Christian determine the value of secular things as having to do with the spiritual life?"

Paul has much to say concerning the believer and separation from the world. Whatever doctrine or truth he sets forth, he always climaxes his teaching by showing its application to the practical matter of separation from the world and its interests. He wanted his children in the Lord to enjoy their spiritual birthright, and at the end of life's journey receive a full reward.

In Romans 12:2 Paul issues a command: *". . . Be not conformed to the world: but be ye transformed by the renewing of your mind, that ye may prove what is that good, and acceptable, and perfect, will of God."*

To the Corinthian Christians he said, "Wherefore, my dearly beloved, flee from idolatry. . . . Be not deceived: evil communications corrupt good manners" (I Cor. 10:14; 15:33).

In II Corinthians 6:14 he admonished, "Be ye not unequally yoked together with unbelievers: for what fellowship hath righteousness with unrighteousness? and what communion hath light with darkness?"

To the believers in Galatia, Paul gave this message: "Grace be to you and peace from God the Father, and from our Lord Jesus Christ, who gave Himself for our sins, that He might deliver us from this present evil world, according to the will of God and our Father" (Gal. 1:4).

To the Ephesians he wrote, "Let no man deceive you with

vain words: for because of these things cometh the wrath of God upon the children of disobedience. Be not ye therefore partakers with them . . . and have no fellowship with the unfruitful works of darkness, but rather reprove them" (Eph. 5:6-11 in part).

Writing to the church at Colosse, he said, ". . . It is God which worketh in you both to will and to do of His good pleasure. Do all things without murmurings and disputings; that ye may be blameless and harmless, the sons of God, without rebuke, in the midst of a crooked and perverse nation, among whom ye shine as lights in the world" (Phil. 2:13-15).

In Colossians 3:1-3 we read, "If ye then be risen with Christ, seek those things which are above, where Christ sitteth on the right hand of God. Set your affection on things above, not on things on the earth. For ye are dead, and your life is hid with Christ in God."

Paul advised the Thessalonians to "prove all things; hold fast that which is good. *Abstain from all appearance of evil*" (I Thess. 5:21, 22).

To Timothy he wrote, *"Flee also youthful lusts*: but follow righteousness, faith, charity, peace, with them that call on the Lord out of a pure heart" (II Tim. 2:22).

In Titus 2:11-14 Paul plainly tells us, "The grace of God that bringeth salvation hath appeared to all men, *teaching us that, denying ungodliness and worldly lusts, we should live soberly, righteously, and godly, in this present world;* looking for that blessed hope, and the glorious appearing of the great God and our Saviour Jesus Christ; who gave Himself for us, that He might redeem us from all iniquity, and purify unto Himself a peculiar people, zealous of good works."

The Prince of Apostles preached the positive Gospel that brings redemption — salvation by grace, through faith, plus nothing; but he also preached the *negative Gospel* to those who had received the positive. The beginning of salvation is positive; but after we are born again, the negatives should be practiced — i.e., "Be not conformed . . . be not deceived . . . be not unequally yoked . . . be not partakers . . . touch not the unclean . . . be ye separate!"

We cannot separate ourselves from society, but we can separate ourselves from the *habits of society*. We are to be separated from all evil, anything that has to do with this present evil world-system. We are not to conform. We are IN the world, we rub shoulders with the world, but we are not to be partakers of the practices of the world. We cannot go into seclusion, because the only way to help people is to mix and mingle with them; but we should do this after the method of Jesus.

When He met the woman of questionable character at Jacob's well, He did not allow her to begin the conversation, but rather, beginning with a request for a drink, He opened the conversation which eventually led to her salvation. The enemies of Jesus accused Him of being a friend of sinners. It is true that he visited in their homes, He ate with them — *but He did not follow their habits of life nor stoop to their level of conduct*. The Lord Jesus Christ, greatest Preacher, Teacher, and Soul-winner ever to walk this earth, was "holy, harmless, undefiled, separate from sinners, and made higher than the heavens" (Heb. 7:26).

Separation from the world is not a self-righteous, "holier-than-thou" attitude. It is, by parallel, as a bride separates herself from all others when she is betrothed to the bridegroom. Believers are betrothed to Christ, in the spiritual sense, and friendship with the world is spiritual adultery against Him. He calls us His "beloved," and He has every right to expect faithfulness from us — complete separation from anything that is against His will and His righteousness.

Worldliness is an enemy to spirituality and spiritual living, and for the Christian to be spiritual, it is imperative that he sever all relations with worldliness:

"Be ye not unequally yoked together with unbelievers: for what fellowship hath righteousness with unrighteousness? and what communion hath light with darkness? And what concord hath Christ with Belial? or what part hath he that believeth with an infidel? And what agreement hath the temple of God with idols? For ye are the temple of the living God; as God hath said, I will dwell in them, and walk in them; and I will be their

God, and they shall be my people. *Wherefore come out from among them, and be ye separate,* saith the Lord, *and touch not the unclean thing; and I will receive you, and will be a Father unto you, and ye shall be my sons and daughters, saith the Lord Almighty'* (II Cor. 6:14-18).

Notice in verse 14 Paul speaks of the *unequal yoke.* The believer should be in the yoke with *Jesus.* He said, "MY yoke is easy, MY burden is light." If we are where we *should* be as Christians, we will not be yoked with the world.

Paul then uses the word "fellowship," pointing out that idols cannot fellowship with Christ, nor can light fellowship with darkness. There must be a complete break between them.

He speaks of *communion.* A living Christ and a dead idol cannot commune. Since the believer is dead to the world and the world is dead to the believer, there can be no fellowship and communion between them.

In verse 15, Paul asks the question, "What *concord* [agreement or harmony] hath Christ with Belial?" There IS no concord there. The believer cannot fellowship with an atheist.

In verse 16 he uses the word "agreement." There is no agreement between the temple of God and the temple of idols. *Believers* are the temple of the living God; He dwells within the heart. We must, therefore, sever all relations with things of the world — we cannot be spiritually minded unless we do.

It is impossible for fellowship and communion to exist between a believer and an atheist, between an idol and Christ, between light and darkness. It is impossible for spirituality and worldliness to be yoked together. There can be no concord or agreement between them.

Paul was in perfect agreement with James 4:4: ". . . Know ye not that the friendship of the world is enmity with God? Whosoever therefore will be a friend of the world is the enemy of God!" The systems of this world have *always* been at enmity with Jesus Christ, and they are therefore at enmity with His children.

To His disciples Jesus said, "If the world hate you, ye know that it hated me before it hated you. If ye were of the world, the world would love his own; but because ye are NOT of the world, but I have chosen you out of the world, therefore the world hateth you" (John 15:18, 19).

In Luke 6:22 He said to them, "Blessed are ye, when men shall hate you, and *when they shall separate you from their company, and shall reproach you, and cast out your name as evil, FOR THE SON OF MAN'S SAKE!"*

The believer who is a friend to the world has surrendered to *self,* because the *new life* within would never crave the things of the world. In Romans 8:5-10 Paul tells us, ". . . They that are after the flesh do mind the things of the flesh; *but they that are after the Spirit the things of the Spirit.* . . . To be carnally minded is death; but to be spiritually minded is life and peace. Because the carnal mind is enmity against God: for it is not subject to the law of God, neither indeed can be. So then they that are in the flesh cannot please God. BUT YE ARE NOT IN THE FLESH, BUT IN THE SPIRIT, if so be that the Spirit of God dwell in you. Now if any man have not the Spirit of Christ, he is none of His. And if Christ be in you, THE BODY IS DEAD BECAUSE OF SIN: BUT THE SPIRIT IS LIFE BECAUSE OF RIGHTEOUSNESS!"

Every born again believer is daily faced with three deadly foes:

1. The flesh in which we live.
2. The world around us.
3. The devil — who walks about, sometimes as a roaring lion, sometimes as an angel of light, whichever is more suitable to the task he is attempting against the believer.

According to James 1:13-15, any love demonstrated for the world or participation in things of the world originates in the flesh-life, not the spiritual life:

"Let no man say when he is tempted, I am tempted of God: for God cannot be tempted with evil, neither tempteth He any man: *But every man is tempted, when he is drawn away of his own lust, and enticed.* Then when lust hath conceived, it bringeth forth sin: and sin, when it is finished, bringeth forth death!'

But God has provided a way of escape from temptation:

"There hath no temptation taken you but such as is common

to man: *but God is faithful, who will not suffer you to be
tempted above that ye are able; but will with the temptation
also make a way to escape,* that ye may be able to bear it"
(I Cor. 10:13).

Commands of the Gospel According to Paul

The believer should be concerned with and mastered by the
realities of eternity. His eye should be singled on the ultimate,
not on the immediate; he should never be in bondage to tem-
poral things. The Christian who spends most of his time thinking of earthly things, planning for things immediately around
him, is not spiritual. He is worldly, and is fast becoming a
slave to earthly things. Believers who are more concerned
about material things than about things eternal are immature;
they are babes in Christ. They need to grow up in things of the
Spirit.

Paul said, "When I was a child, I spake as a child, I understood as a child, I thought as a child: but when I became a
man, I put away childish things" (I Cor. 13:11). It is most
tragic to look upon a little child who does not grow and develop,
but it is an even greater tragedy for a Christian to allow the
things of the world to rob him of his spiritual birthright by
hindering him from growing into spiritual maturity!

The Christian who is more concerned about earthly things
than about things of the spirit will eventually do what Demas
did, as recorded by Paul in II Timothy 4:10: *"Demas hath
forsaken me, having loved this present world, and is departed*
unto Thessalonica. . . ." If the action of Demas wounded the
heart of the Apostle Paul to such degree, think what it must
have done to the heart of the Lord Jesus Christ!

As runners in a race, believers are admonished to lay aside
anything that would hinder:

"Wherefore seeing we also are compassed about with so great
a cloud of witnesses, *let us lay aside every weight, and the
sin which doth so easily beset us, a*nd let us run with patience
the race that is set before us" (Heb. 12:1). Worldliness hinders
the Christian in the race.

In Galatians 4:9 Paul asks, "But now, after that ye have

known God, or rather are known of God, how turn ye again to the weak and beggarly elements, whereunto ye desire again to be in bondage?"

Believers are vessels in which the Holy Spirit abides. If we would be vessels "meet for the Master's use," we must purge ourselves from the things of the world:

"If a man therefore purge himself from these, he shall be a vessel unto honour, sanctified, and meet for the master's use, and prepared unto every good work" (II Tim. 2:21).

To be a spiritually minded Christian is not to be isolated, but rather, to be *insulated.* We have joy within, at God's right hand we have pleasures forever more, He is our sufficiency and we are complete in Him. To the true believer, separation is not a burden, but a joy. By contrast, the believer who becomes entangled with the affairs of this world will be hindered as a runner for Jesus, he will be handicapped as a good soldier in the army of the Lord, he will be a vessel dishonored and unclean, unfit for the Master's use — and he will never be prepared for the good work for which we are created in Christ Jesus!

In the New Testament there are two Greek words which are translated "world." In our *English* Bible they are translated identically, but in the original Greek they have different meanings. The first word is *aion,* meaning "age," and the second word is *kosmos,* meaning "system."

In Romans 12:2 the Greek word is *age*: ". . . Be not conformed to this AGE. . . ." In I Corinthians 2:8, the word is age: ". . . The princes of this age. . . ."

In II Corinthians 4:4, "age" is used again: ". . . The god of this Age . . ." meaning Satan. In Ephesians 6:12, the word again is "age," speaking of the fact that we wrestle not against flesh and blood, "but against principalities, against powers, against the rulers of the darkness of this AGE, against spiritual wickedness in high places."

In II Timothy 4:10 the word is "age," as Paul speaks of Demas forsaking him, "having loved this present AGE."

This is the age of darkness. This is man's day. For six thousand years man has lived upon this earth, during which

God has spoken to him in many and various ways. This day
of grace has been the longest period of time in the history of
man that God has not spoken directly, through personal judgment upon sin — but man's day will come to an end.

This is a dark day, but it is also the day of salvation (II Cor.
6:2). In spite of the darkness of this, man's day, the light of
the glorious Gospel has penetrated the darkness, "and the darkness comprehended it not" (John 1:5). Christ's death on the
cross made salvation possible, even in this dark hour, for all
who will come unto God by Him. Christ "gave Himself for our
sins, that He might deliver us from this present evil world,
according to the will of God and our Father: to whom be
glory for ever and ever. Amen" (Gal. 1:4, 5).

This is the day of darkness — but the day of light is just
ahead, for there is a day coming when the earth will be filled
with the knowledge of the Lord as the waters now cover the
sea (Isa. 11:9). The devil will be in the pit, sealed there for
one thousand glorious years. There will be peace on earth,
good will toward men. (Read Revelation, chapter 20.)

Kosmos, the second Greek word translated "world," means
systems. It is used in I Corinthians 3:19 where Paul speaks
of "the wisdom of this world" — the wisdom of *the systems of
this world.* We must agree that in this field we are having a
repetition of Noah days. There are giants today — *mental*
giants, not exceptionally tall physically but twenty-five feet tall
mentally. These are men of extraordinary wisdom — but instead of using their wisdom to advance the cause of Christ,
they are using it to advance the cause of the *world systems.*
They proclaim over and over again that through their great
wisdom they will eventually bring about *one world,* which will
be a world of peace!

It matters not what man may say about world peace — and
we hear much on the subject today — *lasting peace* will never
be a reality *until King Jesus sits on the throne of David in
Jerusalem.*

Paul uses the word *kosmos* (world systems) in I Corinthians
7:31 — *"the fashion of this world"* — and in Galatians 4:3 where
he speaks of "the *elements* of the world." In Ephesians 6:12 he

uses the same word as applied to the *rulers* of this world, the rulers in the systems of the world, who at this time are seeking to bring about a world government. *This will literally take place* after the Rapture, when the Antichrist takes over the rule of the world.

In Ephesians 2:2 Paul uses *kosmos* in speaking of *"the course of this world"* (or world systems). I think most of us agree that the vast majority of the systems of this world are influenced and dominated by the power of Satan. He has organized the masses of unbelieving humanity, and they operate on the principles of selfishness, pleasure, and greed. They have neither time nor place for God in their program. The systems of this world are elegant, scientific — and outwardly religious. They demonstrate culture, but the heart of it all is dominated by Satanic principles and energized by Satanic power.

I do not hesitate to say that the world systems today — governmental, political, educational — yes, even religiously speaking — are controlled and manipulated by "the god of this age." I do realize that there are born again men in government. There are born again men and women in the educational system of our day, and I thank God for them. Certainly there are born again people in the different religious denominations, some of them in high places. But the *heart* of the world systems today is Satanic — in its outlook and in its planning.

The masses of the world today say they do not *need* God, and the majority of political, religious, scientific, and even *educational* organizations are operating wholly apart from Him. They afford Him no consultations and give Him no credit whatsoever. They are attempting to build Nimrod's tower again.

According to the Apostle Paul, we, as unbelievers, ALL walked according to the course of this world. Our conversation, our conduct, and our behaviour were ordered and dominated by the course of this world. We were in sympathy with the projects, plans, and programs of this world system. We enjoyed their pleasures, accepted their standards, sought after their honors, coveted their awards, and shared their hopes. We agreed with their outlook and judged by their scale of values.

These facts are borne out in the following Scriptures:

"And you hath He quickened, who were dead in trespasses and sins: Wherein in time past ye walked according to the course of this world, according to the prince of the power of the air, the spirit that now worketh in the children of disobedience: Among whom also we all had our conversation in times past in the lusts of our flesh, fulfilling the desires of the flesh and of the mind; and were by nature the children of wrath, even as others" (Eph. 2:1-3).

"For we ourselves also were sometimes foolish, disobedient, deceived, serving divers lusts and pleasures, living in malice and envy, hateful, and hating one another" (Tit. 3:3).

As unbelievers, we were all of these evil things — *"BUT GOD, who is rich in mercy, for His great love wherewith He loved us, even when we were dead in sins, hath quickened us together with Christ . . ."* (Eph. 2:4, 5).

"BUT after that the kindness and love of God our Saviour toward man appeared, not by works of righteousness which we have done, but according to His mercy He saved us, by the washing of regeneration, and renewing of the Holy Ghost; which He shed on us abundantly through Jesus Christ our Saviour; *That being justified by His grace, we should be made heirs according to the hope of eternal life.* This is a faithful saying, and these things I will that thou affirm constantly, that they which have believed in God might be careful to maintain good works. These things are good and profitable unto men" (Tit. 3:4-8).

The princes and the systems of this world crucified our Lord. Therefore, since we are delivered from the systems of the world, translated out of the kingdom of darkness, we should completely sever relations with world-systems and look to Jesus, the author and finisher of our faith, knowing that IN HIM we shall be victorious.

Believers Are Now Citizens of Heaven

"For our conversation [citizenship] is in heaven; from whence also we look for the Saviour, the Lord Jesus Christ: Who shall change our vile body, that it may be fashioned like unto His glorious body, according to the working whereby He is able even to subdue all things unto Himself" (Phil. 3:20, 21).

Positionally, the true believer is as sure for heaven as if he were already there — but please note that I said *the true believer* — covered by the blood, saved by God's grace, partaker of divine nature, indwelt, led, and sealed by the Holy Spirit. I did not say the nominal church member, the *professing* Christian.

We pray, "Our Father, which art in heaven." Our Father IS in heaven (Matt. 6:9).

The *Saviour of our souls* is in heaven, seated at the right hand of God the Father (Heb. 1:1-3; Phil. 3:20).

Our *eternal home* is the Pearly White City (John 14:2; Rev. 21).

Our *life* is in heaven (Col. 3:3), we are but pilgrims and strangers here.

According to the words of Jesus, the *heart* of the believer is in heaven (Matt. 6:19-21).

Our *inheritance* is in heaven (I Pet. 1:4), reserved for us, incorruptible and undefiled, an inheritance that will never fade away. Eventually we will arrive there to enjoy it.

Our glorified bodies are as sure as the Word of the living God:

"For we KNOW that if our earthly house of this tabernacle were dissolved, we have a building of God, an house not made with hands, eternal in the heavens" (II Cor. 5:1).

"Behold, what manner of love the Father hath bestowed upon us, that we should be called the sons of God: therefore the world knoweth us not, because it knew Him not. Beloved, NOW are we the sons of God, and it doth not yet appear what we shall be: but we KNOW that, when He shall appear, we shall be like Him; for we shall see Him as He is!" (I John 3:1-3).

The hope of the believer is in heaven (Col. 1:5). The name of every born again, blood-washed believer is written in heaven (Luke 10:20). The truly born again believer has many reasons not to be concerned about "the weak and beggarly elements" of the world (Gal. 4:9). As Christians, we feed from the Father's table, and having tasted of His provisions, the world's garbage just does not attract!

In Hebrews 11:10 we read that Abraham, *by faith,* sojourned in the land of promise "as in a strange country. . . . For he looked for a city which hath foundations, whose builder and maker is God."

By contrast, Lot — the nephew of Abraham — is a picture of the worldly-minded believer. We cannot deny that Lot was a just man — Peter emphatically declares it to be so (II Pet. 2:7); but while Abraham believed God and served Him, Lot cast his eyes toward social advantages and compromised with the Sodomites. He paid dearly for the choice he made!

You may rest assured of the truth of Romans 14:11: "For it is written, AS I LIVE, saith the Lord, EVERY KNEE SHALL BOW TO ME, AND EVERY TONGUE SHALL CONFESS TO GOD!"

Eternal Rewards Differ

Those who believe and teach that all sons of God will be *rewarded equally* do not know the truth of Scripture. Those who are faithful will receive a FULL reward. Those who are unfaithful will suffer loss:

"Know ye not that they which run in a race run all, but ONE receiveth the prize? So run, that ye may obtain" (I Cor. 9:24).

"Look to yourselves, that we lose not *those things which we have wrought,* but that we receive *a full reward*" (II John 8).

"For other foundation can no man lay than that is laid, which is Jesus Christ. Now if any man build upon this foundation gold, silver, precious stones, wood, hay, stubble; every man's work shall be made manifest: for the day shall declare it, because it shall be revealed by fire; and the fire shall try every man's work of what sort it is. *If any man's work abide which he hath built thereupon, he shall receive a reward. If any man's work shall be burned, he shall suffer loss but he himself shall be saved; yet so as by fire*" (I Cor. 3:11-15).

Paul testified, *"For to me to live is Christ, and to die is gain"*

(Phil. 1:21). We can give the same testimony if we will surrender as he did, and live as he lived.

Believers should live soberly, righteously, and godly in this present world, "looking for that blessed hope, and the glorious appearing of the great God and our Saviour Jesus Christ; Who gave Himself for us, that He might redeem us from all iniquity, and purify unto Himself a peculiar people, zealous of good works" (Tit. 2:13-15).

We should hear the admonition of John the Beloved: "And now, little children, abide in Him; that, when He shall appear, we may have confidence, and not be ashamed before Him at His coming" (I John 2:28).

Every truly born again child of God should be able to testify with Paul, ". . . *God forbid that I should glory, save in the cross of our Lord Jesus Christ, by whom the world is crucified unto me, and I unto the world*" (Gal. 6:14).

> When I survey the wondrous cross,
>   On which the Prince of glory died,
> My richest gain I count but loss,
>   And pour contempt on all my pride.
>
> Forbid it, Lord! that I should boast,
>   Save in the death of Christ, my God;
> All the vain things that charm me most
>   I sacrifice them to His blood.
>
> See, from His head, His hands, His feet,
>   Sorrow and love flow mingled down;
> Did e'er such love and sorrow meet,
>   Or thorns compose so rich a crown?
>
> Were the whole realm of nature mine,
>   That were a present far too small;
> Love so amazing, so divine,
>   Demands my soul, my life, my all!

Chapter IX

The Believer and His Enemies

There are those who think that Christianity is for little folk, sick folk, and old folk who are ready to depart this life — but nothing could be further from the truth. *Anyone* can yield to temptation, serve sin, be led about by the devil, and at the end of life's journey die and go to hell; but it takes a person of character, with determined will and "strong backbone," to say "*No*." One needs no will power in order to yield to the world, the flesh, and the devil.

The Christian life is a battlefield — not a picnic. Christians are on a pilgrimage — not a vacation. We are commanded to "fight the good fight of faith." Hear what Paul has to say about it in I Corinthians 4:9-16:

"*. . . I think that God hath set forth us the apostles last, as it were appointed to death: for we are made a spectacle unto the world, and to angels, and to men. We are fools for Christ's sake, but ye are wise in Christ; we are weak, but ye are strong; ye are honourable, but we are despised. Even unto this present hour we both hunger, and thirst, and are naked, and are buffeted, and have no certain dwellingplace; and labour, working with our own hands: being reviled, we bless; being persecuted, we suffer it; being defamed, we intreat: we are made as the filth of the world, and are the offscouring of all things unto this day.* I write not these things to shame you, but as my beloved sons I warn you. For though ye have ten thousand instructors in Christ, yet have ye not many fathers: for in Christ Jesus I have begotten you through the Gospel. Wherefore I beseech you, be ye followers of me."*

In II Corinthians 11:23-28 Paul gives a personal testimony

of the persecution that was heaped upon him as a minister of the Gospel:

". . . In stripes above measure, in prisons more frequent, in deaths oft. Of the Jews five times received I forty stripes save one. Thrice was I beaten with rods, once was I stoned, thrice I suffered shipwreck, a night and a day I have been in the deep. In journeyings often, in perils of waters, in perils of robbers, in perils by mine own countrymen, in perils by the heathen, in perils in the city, in perils in the wilderness, in perils in the sea, in perils among false brethren; in weariness and painfulness, in watchings often, in hunger and thirst, in fastings often, in cold and nakedness. Besides those things that are without, that which cometh upon me daily, the care of all the churches!"

In testimony relating to his ministry, Paul said, ". . . In all things approving ourselves as the ministers of God, in much patience, in afflictions, in necessities, in distresses, in stripes, in imprisonments, in tumults, in labours, in watchings, in fastings; by pureness, by knowledge, by longsuffering, by kindness, by the Holy Ghost, by love unfeigned, by the Word of truth, by the power of God, by the armour of righteousness on the right hand and on the left, by honour and dishonour, by evil report and good report: as deceivers, and yet true; as unknown, and yet well known; as dying, and, behold, we live; as chastened, and not killed; as sorrowful, yet alway rejoicing; as poor, yet making many rich; as having nothing, and yet possessing all things" (II Cor. 6:4-10).

In II Corinthians 12:10 Paul said, ". . . I take pleasure in infirmities, in reproaches, in necessities, in persecutions, in distresses for Christ's sake: for when I am weak, then am I strong."

This Prince of Apostles enjoined young Timothy, his son in the ministry, to "endure hardness, as a good soldier of Jesus Christ" (II Tim. 2:3). And Paul practiced what he preached. Near the end of his earthly life, as he sat in the death-house of a Roman prison, knowing that his execution could be but days — perhaps even hours — away, he wrote this soul-searching testimony to Timothy: *"I am now ready to be offered, and the time of my departure is at hand. I have fought a good fight; I*

*have finished my course, I have kept the faith: Henceforth there
is laid up for me a crown of righteousness, which the Lord, the
righteous Judge, shall give me at that day* — and not to me only,
but unto all them also that love His appearing" (II Tim. 4:6-8).

Here was a devoted, dedicated apostle who many times
hazarded his very life for the sake of the Gospel: ". . . *Neither
count I my life dear unto myself, so that I might finish my
course with joy, and the ministry, which I have received of
the Lord Jesus, to testify the Gospel of the grace of God"*
(Acts 20:24).

The more Paul was persecuted, the more dedicated he became. The more he suffered, the more he served. He had two
types of enemies, as do believers today: (1) *The powers of
darkness* — wicked spirits, demons; and (2) *the Christ-re-
jecting world.* He suffered many times and to great degree
from both — from *without* he was attacked by enemies from
the human standpoint, and from *within* he was attacked by
the Satanic forces.

Human Enemies

The greater percentage of Paul's human enemies came from
the religious sects of that day — scribes, Pharisees, chief priests,
rulers in the synagogue. Throughout his missionary journeys
he was constantly under fire from this opposition. The enemies of the Gospel followed him as a hound follows a fox in
the chase. There was no secret about the mistreatment he
received at their hands in the cities where he preached the
Gospel of grace — and where, more often than not, he was
used of the Lord to establish local assemblies.

We are told that just after his conversion, he "straightway
preached Christ in the synagogues, that He is the Son of God"
(Acts 9:20). This did not please the Jews, because they
believed Jesus to have been a child of fornication, an illegiti-
mate religious imposter. Just after Paul delivered his first sermon, the Jews in Damascus were so enraged that they took
counsel to kill him, "But their laying await was known of Saul.
And they watched the gates day and night to kill him. Then

the disciples took him by night, and let him down by the wall in a basket" (Acts 9:23-25).

Paul did not soft-pedal the Gospel when he began preaching in Jerusalem: "He spake boldly in the name of the Lord Jesus, and disputed against the Grecians: *but they went about to slay him.* Which when the brethren knew, they brought him down to Caesarea, and sent him forth to Tarsus" (Acts 9:29, 30).

In Antioch, Paul had successful meetings among the Gentiles. They responded to his preaching of the glorious Gospel of grace, the good news that Jesus saves; but again, his own brethren the Jews attacked him:

"But when the Jews saw the multitudes, they were filled with envy, and spake against those things which were spoken by Paul, contradicting and blaspheming. Then Paul and Barnabas waxed bold, and said, *It was necessary that the Word of God should first have been spoken to YOU:* but seeing ye put it from you, and judge yourselves unworthy of everlasting life, lo, we turn to the Gentiles. For so hath the Lord commanded us, saying, I have set thee to be a light of the Gentiles, that thou shouldest be for salvation unto the ends of the earth. And when the Gentiles heard this, they were glad, and glorified the Word of the Lord: and as many as were ordained to eternal life believed. And the Word of the Lord was published throughout all the region. *But the Jews stirred up the devout and honourable women, and the chief men of the city, and raised persecution against Paul and Barnabas, and expelled them out of their coasts"* (Acts 13:45-50).

From thence Paul traveled to Iconium where he again preached the message of Jesus Christ — the Son of God, crucified, buried, risen:

"But the unbelieving Jews stirred up the Gentiles, and made their minds evil affected against the brethren. Long time therefore abode they speaking boldly in the Lord, which gave testimony unto the Word of His grace, and granted signs and wonders to be done by their hands. But the multitude of the city was divided: and part held with the Jews, and part with the apostles. And *when there was an assault made both of the Gentiles, and also of the Jews with their rulers, to use*

*them despitefully, and to stone them, they were ware of it,
and fled unto Lystra and Derbe,* cities of Lycaonia, and unto
the region that lieth round about: AND THERE THEY
PREACHED THE GOSPEL" (Acts 14:2-7).

But in the city of Lystra, the persecution by the Jews became even more severe:

*"And there came thither certain Jews from Antioch and
Iconium, who persuaded the people, and, having stoned Paul,
drew him out of the city, supposing he had been dead"*
(Acts 14:19).

It is common belief among Bible scholars that this was the
time of Paul's experience as recorded in II Corinthians 12:1-4.
They believe that the apostle actually *was dead*: but the saints
who loved him so dearly gathered 'round him and prayed,
and God raised him from the dead.

Acts 16 records Paul's experience in Philippi. Lydia, a seller
of purple, lady of the elite, was his first convert in Europe;
and after her conversion at the ladies' prayermeeting where
Paul preached the Gospel, she invited the men of God to come
into her house and abide there. Thus, Paul moved into the
city, preaching Christ.

Under his preaching a fortune-teller was converted, and
those who used this girl for greedy gain were very angry
because they saw that their hope of gain was gone. They
had Paul and Silas arrested, beaten, and thrown into prison,
securely locked in the inner cell, their feet fastened in stocks.

But though these men were locked in prison, they knew a
Saviour who could not be locked out! And at midnight, as
Paul and Silas sang and praised God, the walls of the prison
were rocked by a great earthquake as God answered their
prayers. The prison doors were opened, chains were loosed,
and the prisoners were set free. Thus what outwardly had
seemed a tragedy, God turned into a great victory. Revival
broke out, a jailer was saved, together with his entire household! And from this nucleus, the church at Philippi was established.

In the flourishing city of Thessalonica the Jews became so
angry at the message of grace as preached by the Apostle Paul

that they turned the entire city into an uproar against him:
"And the brethren immediately sent away Paul and Silas by
night, unto Berea . . ." (Acts 17:10).

Here, too, in spite of the great results of the Gospel Paul
preached and the fact that many believed on the Lord Jesus
Christ, "when the Jews of Thessalonica had knowledge that the
Word of God was preached of Paul at Berea, they came thither
also, and stirred up the people. And then immediately the
brethren sent away Paul to go as it were to the sea: but
Silas and Timotheus abode there still" (Acts 17:13, 14).

Moving into the city of Athens, the apostle again met with
persecution. He was mocked, he was called a "babbler," and
after preaching his sermon from Mars' Hill, "Paul departed
from among them" (Acts 17:17-33).

From Athens he moved into Corinth — and the Jews were
ready for him. They hated him, they despised his message.
They therefore "made insurrection with one accord against
Paul, and brought him to the judgment seat" (Acts 18:12).

In the city of Ephesus, center of worship of the goddess
Diana, persecution was severe. Paul's preaching of the Gospel
had affected the income of the silversmiths and craftsmen
who made silver shrines for Diana, and among them "there
arose no small stir." The city was filled with confusion, the
people were "full of wrath" against the apostle. Read the
account in Acts 19 — the entire chapter.

After the episode in Ephesus, Paul returned to the city of
Jerusalem, even though he well knew that further persecution
awaited him there:

"And now, behold, I go bound in the spirit unto Jerusalem,
not knowing the things that shall befall me there, *save that
the Holy Ghost witnesseth in every city, saying that bonds
and afflictions abide me*" (Acts 20:22, 23).

This Prince of Apostles clearly believed that "if God be for
us, who can be against us?" He did not turn aside or turn
back when danger threatened. He believed in obeying God
rather than man. It was he who proclaimed the blessed
truth of Romans 8:28: "We know that all things work together
for good to them that love God, to them who are the called

according to his purpose." So he moved into the city of Jerusalem and began his ministry, preaching Jesus Christ, the Son of God, crucified, buried, risen.

He preached in the temple, and the Jews, when they saw him in the temple, "stirred up all the people, and laid hands on him, crying out, Men of Israel, help: This is the man that teacheth all men every where against the people, and the law, and this place: and further brought Greeks also into the temple, and hath polluted this holy place . . . and all the city was moved and the people ran together: and they took Paul, and drew him out of the temple . . . and *as they went about to kill him,* tidings came unto the chief captain of the band, that all Jerusalem was in an uproar. Who immediately took soldiers and centurions, and ran down unto them: *and when they saw the chief captain and the soldiers, they left beating of Paul"* (Acts 21:27-32 in part).

They then bound him with two chains, and even though they allowed him to give his testimony, that did not end his persecution. The Jews hated him so violently, and so determined were they to put an end to him, that more than forty Jews banded together, "and bound themselves under a curse, saying that they would neither eat nor drink till they had killed Paul . . . And they came to the chief priests and elders, and said, We have bound ourselves under a great curse, that we will eat nothing until we have slain Paul. Now therefore ye with the council signify to the chief captain that he bring him down unto you tomorrow, as though ye would enquire something more perfectly concerning him: and we, or ever he come near, are ready to kill him" (Acts 23:12-15).

But Paul's nephew heard of the plot, and made haste to report his findings to the apostle and in turn to the chief captain, who immediately summoned a heavy guard of soldiers, horsemen, and spearmen and under cover of night had Paul spirited away to Caesarea, where the governor commanded him to be kept in Herod's judgment hall. You will find the account in Acts 23:16-35.

It was here that Paul made his great confession and gave his moving testimony before Festus, Felix, and Agrippa — his testi-

mony of the experience he had in his meeting with the Christ on
the Damascus road. So effective was his message that at its
close King Agrippa said, *"Almost thou persuadest ME to be a
Christian!"* (Acts 26:28).

Since Paul was a Roman citizen, he had appealed to Caesar,
and in response to that appeal he was ordered sent to Rome to
appear before Caesar. He traveled by sea, and the twenty-
seventh chapter of Acts gives the account of that journey, with
its subsequent shipwreck and Paul's ministry on the island of
Melita where he performed miracles of healing among the people there. (Read also Acts 28:1-10.)

Paul finally reached Rome, and "the centurion delivered the
prisoners to the captain of the guard; but Paul was suffered to
dwell by himself with a soldier that kept him" (Acts 28:16).

In Acts 28:30, 31 we read, *"And Paul dwelt two whole years
in his own hired house, and received all that came in unto him,
preaching the kingdom of God, and teaching those things which
concern the Lord Jesus Christ, with all confidence, no man for-
bidding him!"*

In spite of the guards which were with him day and night, he
daily preached the grace of God — and who can say how many
of those guards were touched, perhaps converted, by his message? There is always opportunity for a believer to tell forth the
good news that Jesus saves!

I know that all Scripture is inspired, verbally dictated to
holy men of old who penned down the words the Holy Spirit
gave them, but I am especially thankful that Paul could give us
the tremendous words of Romans 8:35-39 — not only from inspiration, but from personal experience:

"Who shall separate us from the love of Christ? Shall tribulation, or distress, or persecution, or famine or nakedness, or
peril, or sword? As it is written, For thy sake we are killed all
the day long; we are accounted as sheep for the slaughter. Nay,
in all these things we are more than conquerors through Him
that loved us. *For I am persuaded, that neither death, nor life,
nor angels, nor principalities, nor powers, nor things present,
nor things to come, nor height, nor depth, nor any other creature,*

shall be able to separate us from the love of God, which is in Christ Jesus our Lord!"

(I ask you: *Who, among ordinary men,* could have been more qualified to utter those words? No wonder he said to the Philippians, "For me to live is Christ, *to die is gain!"*

The devil and hell have not produced — neither has the world manufactured — the power that can sever us from the love of God which is in Christ Jesus our Lord. The truth set forth here was not only Paul's *conviction* — it was his *experience* as well. He had been tried, tested, attacked from all angles by all things. He knew that believers are not merely conquerors, but that we are MORE than conquerors — THROUGH HIM that loved us.

Romans 8 is one of the most beloved chapters in all of the Word of God. It begins in Christ Jesus ("There is therefore now no condemnation to them which are *IN Christ Jesus*") and ends in Christ Jesus (". . . nor any other creature, shall be able to separate us from the love of God, which is IN CHRIST JESUS OUR LORD"), just as *saving faith* begins in Jesus, continues in Jesus, and climaxes in Jesus.

When Jesus tabernacled among men, preaching, healing, and teaching, He did not promise His disciples an easy road. Quite the contrary. He said, "Behold, I send you forth as sheep in the midst of wolves: be ye therefore wise as serpents, and harmless as doves. But beware of men: for they will deliver you up to the councils, and they will scourge you in their synagogues; and ye shall be brought before governors and kings for my sake . . . and the brother shall deliver up the brother to death, and the father the child: and the children shall rise up against their parents, and cause them to be put to death. And ye shall be hated of all men for my name's sake. . . . Think not that I am come to send peace on earth: I came not to send peace, but a sword. For I am come to set a man at variance against his father, the daughter against her mother, and the daughter-in-law against her mother-in-law, and a man's foes shall be they of his own household. He that loveth father or mother more than me is not worthy of me: and he that loveth son or daughter more than me is not worthy of me. And he that taketh not his cross, and followeth after me, is not worthy of me. He that findeth his life shall lose it: and he that loseth his life for my sake shall find it" (Matt. 10:16-39 in part).

Jesus did not say, "Follow me — and I will give you a mansion to live in, I will put a big automobile in your garage, I will have all men speak well of you and give you a promotion every six months!" On the contrary, He promised trials, testings, persecutions, a cross to bear — and, for many, *martyrdom*.

Of Christ Paul said, "For it became Him, for whom are all things, and by whom are all things, in bringing many sons unto glory, to make the Captain of their salvation perfect through sufferings" (Heb. 2:10). In Hebrews 5:8 he said, "Though He were a Son, yet learned He obedience by the things which He suffered."

If we fall victim to the world, the flesh, and the devil, we have no one to blame but ourselves. The Captain of our salvation overcame, and *He promised us* the power to overcome — He promised to make a way of escape for us. In his death He *conquered* death, hell, and the grave. Seated at the right hand of God the Father to make intercession for us, He now lives to die no more.

Victory is not cheap — it cost Jesus His life's blood. But there can be no conquest without conflict. There can be no victory without valor. We should be good soldiers of Jesus Christ — soldiers who refuse to retreat or yield ground. The hotter the battle, the more we should tighten our armor and wield the sword of the Spirit, determined to march on to victory! The life that counts *for* Christ is the life fully dedicated *to* Christ. From the standpoint of the world, it will be costly — but it will pay tremendous dividends in the world to come.

Spiritual Enemies

The devil's first desire is to damn the soul; but if an individual trusts Jesus unto salvation, thereby becoming a child of God, Satan does not give up. He simply marshalls his forces and declares all-out war on the believer in an attempt to hinder his being a good soldier, a good runner, a good steward or servant of the Christ who saved him!

There will be Satanic conflicts. We will be called upon to

battle the powers of darkness. Paul describes these Satanic enemies in Ephesians 6:10-18:

"Finally, my brethren, be strong in the Lord, and in the power of His might. Put on the whole armour of God, that ye may be able to stand against the wiles of the devil. For we wrestle not against flesh and blood, but against principalities, against powers, against the rulers of the darkness of this world, against spiritual wickedness in high places.

"Wherefore take unto you the whole armour of God, that ye may be able to withstand in the evil day, and having done all, to stand. Stand therefore, having your loins girt about with truth, and having on the breastplate of righteousness; and your feet shod with the preparation of the Gospel of peace; above all, taking the shield of faith, wherewith ye shall be able to quench all the fiery darts of the wicked. And take the helmet of salvation, and the sword of the Spirit, which is the Word of God: Praying always with all prayer and supplication in the Spirit, and watching thereunto with all perseverance and supplication for all saints!"

This battle is much more deadly than that between the Christian and his human enemies; it is in the realm of the supernatural, against invisible foes. From the moment one becomes a believer until he is safe in the Paradise of God, his journey will be across a bloody battlefield, against powers mobilized by Satanic forces. This is no ordinary fight. Paul advises the Christian to put on the *whole* armour of God in order to be able to stand:

AGAINST the wiles of the devil,

AGAINST principalities,

AGAINST powers,

AGAINST the rulers of darkness,

AGAINST spiritual wickedness in high places.

This is no tangible enemy, he is not flesh and blood; but he is powerful, insidious, subtle, evil, more ingenious and much more to be feared than any human foe.

Paul refers to the devil in various terms, but always in a tone of warning:

"Lest Satan should get an advantage of us: for we are not ignorant of his *devices*" (II Cor. 2:11).

In the Scripture just quoted from Ephesians, he speaks of "the *wiles of the devil.*"

In II Timothy 2:26 he says, "And that they may recover themselves out of the *snare* of the devil, who are taken captive by him at his will."

In I Timothy 4:1, 2, he speaks of *"seducing spirits, and doctrines of devils."*

In II Timothy 3:13 he says ". . . *Evil men and seducers shall* wax worse and worse, deceiving, and being deceived."

"But I fear, lest by any means, as *the serpent beguiled Eve* through his subtilty, so your minds should be corrupted from the simplicity that is in Christ . . . For such are false apostles, deceitful workers, transforming themselves into the apostles of Christ. And no marvel: for *Satan himself is transformed into an angel of light.* Therefore it is no great thing if his ministers also be transformed as the ministers of righteousness; whose end shall be according to their works" (II Cor. 11:3, 13-15).

In Ephesians 2:2 Paul refers to *"the prince of the power of the air, the spirit that now worketh in the children of disobedience."*

In II Thessalonians 2:8-10 he said, "And then shall that *Wicked* be revealed, whom the Lord shall consume with the spirit of His mouth, and shall destroy with the brightness of His coming: Even him, whose coming is after the working of Satan with all power and signs and lying wonders, and with all deceivableness of unrighteousness in them that perish; because they received not the love of the truth, that they might be saved."

To the Thessalonians he wrote, "Wherefore we would have come unto you, even I Paul, once and again; *but Satan hindered us"* (I Thess. 2:18).

To the Corinthian Christians he wrote, "For a great door and effectual is opened unto me, and there are many *adversaries"* (I Cor. 16:9).

From these passages from God's Word we can agree that Satan and his cohorts are deceptive, subtle, destructive, and powerful — *but hear this* as Paul speaks of the Saviour:

". . .YOU, being dead in your sins and the uncircumcision of your flesh, *hath He quickened together with HIM,* having for-

given you all trespasses: blotting out the handwriting of or-
dinances that was against us, which was contrary to us, and took
it out of the way, *nailing it to his cross*; *and HAVING SPOILED
PRINCIPALITIES AND POWERS, HE MADE SHEW OF
THEM OPENLY, TRIUMPHING OVER THEM IN IT"*
(Col. 2:13-15).

Beloved, the devil is mighty — *but God is ALMIGHTY!* The
devil is deceptive — but he is not invincible. Jesus met him face
to face, *and defeated him!* Satan is already a defeated foe. Oh,
yes, he is still in operation, but his days are numbered; and one
day Jesus will personally supervise putting him into the lake of
fire.

But many believers tend to become careless. They know they
are saved by grace and kept by the power of God, and they
forget that Satan is more than an "influence." He is very real,
and he never lets up. He comes as a roaring lion, or he comes as
an angel of light, depending upon the approach he deems best
for his own purpose. He is always alert, seeking some way, some
method, by which to cripple the testimony of the child of God.

Still other Christians give the devil TOO MUCH credit. They
live in constant fear that he will overtake them and cause them
to stumble. They fail to realize that they are indwelt by the
Holy Spirit, and therefore greater is He who indwells them
than he who is without. We should never minimize the power
of Satan, but by like token we should never *magnify* his power.
For all of the power he has, GOD is ALL-powerful, and every
believer has the divine nature of God within his heart. WE are
no match for the devil, but the Lord Jesus is MORE than a
match for him. Thus, when the devil comes to the door of our
hearts, we should always send Jesus to the door — and Satan
will take flight!

The source of the Christian's strength is wholly (and ONLY)
in the Lord. We are not strong within ourselves, but we are to
remember that it is ours to be "strong in the Lord, and in the
power of His might." HE won the victory over all the powers
of hell, and IN HIM victory is ours!

Paul speaks of this power in Ephesians 1:18-23:

"The eyes of your understanding being enlightened; that ye

may know what is the hope of His calling, and what the riches of the glory of His inheritance in the saints, *and what is the exceeding greatness of His power to us-ward who believe, according to the working of His mighty power, which He wrought in Christ, when He raised Him from the dead, and set Him at His own right hand in the heavenly places, far above all principality, and power, and might, and dominion, and every name that is named, not only in this world, but also in that which is to come*: And hath put all things under His feet, and gave Him to be the head over all things to the Church, which is His body, the fulness of Him that filleth all in all."

It is by the power which *His supreme might* imparts that we are made strong to resist the tempter — the same power that operated when Jesus broke the bonds of death and rose in victory! Our part is to abide in Him; we are strong only in the Lord, victorious so long as we are kept by His power.

Union between Christ and the believer is a divine imperative if we are to claim the sure guarantee of victory. Moment by moment we are kept — not only IN HIM, but BY HIS POWER. "Strong in the Lord, and in the power of His might," the believer is secure.

You will note that we are told to put on the WHOLE armor of God, and the whole armor consists of the girdle of truth, the breastplate of righteousness, the shoes of the Gospel, the shield of faith, and the helmet of salvation. With that, we are to take the sword of the Spirit, "which is the Word of God."

No armor is provided for the *back!* Sufficient equipment is provided to win the victory *so long as we face the enemy.* Soldiers in the army of the Lord must never turn their backs to the enemy. We must face him and fight him, always bearing in mind that Jesus is our Commander-in-Chief, and under His directions we will win the victory.

The Christian wears the girdle of truth, which is our perfect defense against Satan's lies. Jesus said to Thomas, "*I am the Truth.*" The devil is The Lie, and the father of lies. After the Rapture, God will send strong delusions and people will *believe* The Lie.

Every error being taught today is of the devil. He hates the truth, he wants to lead the child of God *away* from the truth, he attempts to mix error *with* truth in order to divert the Christian from the truth and thus confuse him. The only way to shut the devil's mouth is with the Word of God: ". . . Thy Word is Truth" (John 17:17).

The believer wears the breastplate of righteousness — guaranteed protection against every subtle effort of the devil to debase us. Satan takes great joy in leading a believer to compromise with evil, to live an inconsistent life, to dwell on the borderline of tolerance, to keep company with questionable friends. If he is successful in this, he thus hinders our effectiveness as stewards and soldiers, causing us to bring reproach upon the name of Jesus. He works untiringly to persuade the Christian to lower standards, forget principles, and become satisfied to compromise in order to avoid hurting friends, losing business, or sacrificing social position.

The Christian as a soldier, or as one running a race, needs good, efficient footwear. God furnishes every believer with the shoes of the Gospel of peace — the guarantee of victory in the race and in the battle: ". . . How beautiful are the feet of them that preach the Gospel of peace and bring glad tidings of good things" (Rom. 10:15).

The Christian wears the shield of faith — protection beyond penetration. It is our safeguard against every suggestion of unbelief on the part of Satan. His fiery darts cannot pierce it.

Unbelief is the root of all sin. "The sin that doth so easily beset us" (Heb. 12:1) is the sin of unbelief. They who come to God must believe that He IS, they who labor for God must labor in faith, for "whatsoever is NOT of faith is sin!" *The just* shall LIVE by faith, and faith is the victory that overcomes the world. No shot or shell from hell's cannons can pierce the shield of faith — part of the armor God supplies for every believer.

The Christian wears the helmet of salvation, which is our perfect, flawless covering against every storm of temptation that would sweep us into discouragement, or cause us to become dismayed or depressed. He who wears the helmet of salvation is watching, waiting, yearning, and praying for the return of our Lord. In such an attitude, the believer lives above the world, he lives in a sphere of the eternal. Our affections should be set on things above, and the more lightly we cling to earth, the tighter our grip on things eternal.

IN CHRIST, *complete* victory lies ahead. We know not the day nor the hour, but we DO KNOW that He is coming, and we are comforted in this assurance. Wearing the helmet of salvation we should always be looking "for that blessed hope, and the glorious appearing of our Lord and Saviour, Jesus Christ."

God furnishes every believer with the sword of the Spirit — the Word of God — with which he can stop or destroy every enemy hell hurls at his soul! When Jesus was baptized of John in the river Jordan, the Spirit immediately led Him into the wilderness to be tempted of the devil. (The record is found in Matthew 4:1-11.) And to every temptation Jesus answered Satan by saying, "*It is written . . .!*" Those words will put the devil to flight. He knows the Word of God is the sword that will defeat him in any battle.

Beloved, *if the devil could discredit the Word of God, he could undermine Christianity!* But the Word is forever settled in heaven, it cannot be destroyed by Satan, it cannot be corrupted. In this day, the devil is doing all in his power to discredit and undermine our faith in the Word of God. He puts a question mark around the *inspiration* of the Word. He attempts in every way possible to destroy the faith of the masses in the Bible as the inspired, holy, Word of God. But regardless of what he may do or say, the Word of God will be standing when the world is on fire and Satan is in the pit!

What glorious armor the Lord has provided for the Christian soldier! Fellow believer, let us *put on* the whole armor of God and do loyal battle for Him IN WHOM we have the victory!

The Lord Jesus Christ is our equipment: He is our light and our salvation — whom shall we fear? (Psalm 27:1). He is our peace (Eph. 2:14). He is the Way, the Truth, and the Life (John 14:6). He is our righteousness (I Cor. 1:30). He is the author and finisher of our faith (Heb. 12:2).

Paul outlines the Christian armor — piece by piece, and commands the believer to *put on* the whole armor — but at the climax of the passage he does not say that we are to be always fighting with courage, nor that we are to be always advancing; but he DOES say that we are to be "PRAYING always, with all prayer and supplication in the Spirit, and watching thereunto with all perseverance and supplication for all saints" (Eph. 6:18).

The apostle is quite sure of the invincibility of the armor which God furnishes for the believer. But he is equally sure that we must keep in touch with God through prayer, communing and fellowshipping with Him, if the armor is to be as effective as it should be. Paul had much to say about prayer. The prayerless Christian is a defeated Christian. In I Thessalonians 5:17 we are enjoined to *"pray without ceasing."* The victorious Christian prays at all times, in all seasons, concerning all things.

But we must also WATCH as we pray. We must be alert and sober because our adversary the devil is always seeking some way to ensnare us. We must guard our conversation and our associations. We must be watchful in our interests, in our social activities, in business, in whatsoever we do. Jesus said, "Watch and pray, lest ye enter into temptation," and if *Jesus* warned concerning prayer as a safeguard against temptation, we should certainly hear His words of admonition and obey them.

Chapter X

The Believer and His Commission

It is a grand and glorious privilege to be a child of God and bear the name "Christian." But just so grand and glorious the privilege, so great and weighty the responsibility. In the sense of evangelism, we are our brother's keeper. The tragedy of tragedies is for a believer to live and work beside unbelievers, rub shoulders with them, but never try to lead them to Christ. This is the most cruel sin man can commit against his fellowman.

It is our responsibility to tell others about the Saviour who saved us. All unbelievers are blind, they are bound in the shackles of sin, they are led about by the devil; and we should attempt to rescue them through the message of salvation: ". . . If our Gospel be hid, it is hid to them that are lost: In whom the god of this world hath blinded the minds of them which believe not, lest the light of the glorious Gospel of Christ, who is the image of God, should shine unto them" (II Cor. 4:3, 4).

Paul declared, "I am debtor both to the Greeks, and to the Barbarians; both to the wise, and to the unwise. So, as much as in me is, I am ready to preach the Gospel. . . . For I am not ashamed of the Gospel of Christ; for it is the power of God unto salvation to every one that believeth; to the Jew first, and also to the Greek. For therein is the righteousness of God revealed from faith to faith: as it is written, The just shall live by faith" (Rom. 1:14-17 in part).

Paul recognized the debt he owed to unbelievers — a debt to preach the Gospel and make known to them the wonderful salvation that *he* had received in Damascus. He recognized his responsibility to make known to others the Gospel of God's saving grace that had meant so much to *him.*

Throughout his epistles, Paul emphasizes the fact that the Christian not only has the grand and glorious *privilege* of telling others about the Saviour, but that he has a great and weighty *responsibility* to do so. In his letter to the Corinthian church he said, ". . . My beloved brethren, *be ye stedfast, unmoveable, always abounding in the work of the Lord,* forasmuch as ye know that your labour is not in vain in the Lord" (I Cor. 15:58).

To Timothy he wrote: "These things command and teach. Let no man despise thy youth; but be thou an example of the believers, in word, in conversation, in charity, in spirit, in faith, in purity. Till I come, give attendance to reading, to exhortation, to doctrine. Neglect not the gift that is in thee, which was given thee by prophecy, with the laying on of the hands of the presbytery. Meditate upon these things; give thyself wholly to them; that thy profiting may appear to all. Take heed unto thyself, and unto the doctrine; continue in them: for in doing this thou shalt both save thyself, and them that hear thee" (I Tim. 4:11-16).

In II Timothy 4:1-5 he continues: "I charge thee therefore before God, and the Lord Jesus Christ, who shall judge the quick and the dead at His appearing and His kingdom: Preach the word; be instant in season, out of season; reprove, rebuke, exhort with all longsuffering and doctrine. For the time will come when they will not endure sound doctrine; but after their own lusts shall they heap to themselves teachers, having itching ears; and they shall turn away their ears from the truth, and shall be turned unto fables. *But watch thou in all things, endure afflictions, do the work of an evangelist, make full proof of thy ministry.*"

In each of these passages of Scripture, Paul earnestly pleads for the spirit of evangelism to be demonstrated, that each believer should *possess and practice* the spirit of evangelism in consistent soul-winning.

The Lord Jesus Christ, greatest soul-winner who ever lived, never passed up an opportunity to witness — even to one individual. To His disciples He said, "My meat is to do the will of Him that sent me, and to finish His work. Say not ye, There are yet four months, and then cometh harvest? *Behold, I say unto you, Lift up your eyes, and look on the fields; for they are white already to harvest.* And he that reapeth receiveth wages, and gathereth fruit unto life eternal: that both he that soweth and he that reapeth may rejoice together" (John 4:34-36).

All we need do today is look around us, listen to the conversation of the masses of humanity, and we will see that the fields are indeed white unto harvest — and as we look upon the reapers we will see that they are few! Today as never before we need to pray for the Lord to send forth laborers into the fields. We should be willing to say, "Lord, here am I! Send ME!'

"The fruit of the righteous is a tree of life; and *he that winneth souls is wise*" (Prov. 11:30).

"*And they that be wise* [soul-winners] *shall shine as the brightness of the firmament; and they that turn many to righteousness as the stars for ever and ever*" (Dan. 12:3).

There is no scriptural basis for the song "Will There Be Any Stars in My Crown?" but the Bible clearly teaches something much better: We will not have stars in our crowns — but if we are faithful soul-winners *we will shine as the brightness of the stars!*

Paul's Message to the Corinthians

"And I, brethren, when I came to you, came not with excellency of speech or of wisdom, declaring unto you the testimony of God. *For I determined not to know anything among you, save Jesus Christ, and Him crucified.* And I was with you in weakness, and in fear, and in much trembling. And my speech and my preaching was not with enticing words of man's wisdom, but in demonstration of the Spirit and of power; *that your faith should not stand in the wisdom of men, but in the power of God*" (I Cor. 2:1-5).

There is a scriptural way to evangelize and win souls. Every believer should be an evangelist in that he gives out the good news that Jesus saves and the grace of God is sufficient. Paul was one of the best educated men of his day, yet he was careful to preach the Gospel in plain, simple language. He wanted his converts to have faith in *the Christ* of the Gospel and trust in His shed blood rather than being influenced by the apostle's speech and enticing words. With his education and background Paul was capable of speaking great swelling words, enticing words that would demonstrate man's wisdom and accomplishments — but he did not preach after that fashion. His message was singular — it was the heart, soul, and essence of salvation: *the cross, Jesus Christ crucified.*

Later in the same epistle he reminds the Corinthian Christians WHY they are believers:

"Moreover, brethren, I declare unto you the Gospel which I preached unto you, which also ye have received, and wherein ye stand; by which also ye are saved, if ye keep in memory what I preached unto you, unless ye have believed in vain. For I delivered unto you first of all that which I also received, how that Christ died for our sins according to the Scriptures; and that He was buried, and that He rose again the third day according to the Scriptures; And that He was seen of Cephas, then of the twelve: After that, He was seen of above five hundred brethren at once; of whom the greater part remain unto this present, but some are fallen asleep. After that, He was seen of James: then of all the apostles. And last of all He was seen of me also, as of one born out of due time. For I am the least of the apostles, that am not meet to be called an apostle, because I persecuted the Church of God. But by the grace of God I am what I am: and His grace which was bestowed upon me was not in vain; but I laboured more abundantly than they all; yet not I, but the grace of God which was with me. Therefore whether it were I or they, so we preach, and so ye believed" (I Cor. 15:1-11).

Notice that Paul reminds the Corinthians that he delivered to them the message which he had first RECEIVED, and it was this message whereby they were saved, and wherein they stood. He preached the blood of Jesus Christ as the only remission for sin — and beloved, any minister who does not preach the virgin birth, the blood atonement, the second coming and the verbal inspiration of the Bible has only one reason for not doing so: If he does not preach these great fundamentals of the faith, then *he does not BELIEVE them!* He will preach what he believes, and if he does not preach these tremendous truths, it is a sure sign that he does not *believe* the truth.

Paul gives here a clear, concise definition of the Gospel. He said "I preach to you what I myself received — first, that *Christ died* for our sins 'according to the Scriptures'; second, *He was buried* 'according to the Scriptures'; third, *He rose again the third day* exactly as the Scriptures said He would. He was seen by His disciples — singly, in groups, and at one time by as many as five hundred." He ascended into heaven after having finished the work He came to do — and that finished work so completely satisfied the heart of God that Christ is now in the highest seat of heaven — at the right hand of God the Father (Heb. 1:1-3).

The fifteenth chapter of I Corinthians is one of the greatest "resurrection" chapters in the entire Bible — and if there BE no resurrection, then all else is empty and vain. If Christ be not raised, then our preaching is vain, our faith is vain, and our loved ones who have died in the Lord are lost forever.

". . . *If ye keep in memory what I preached unto you* . . ." (v. 2). Paul is here reminding the believers in Corinth that the cross of the Lord Jesus Christ and the bodily resurrection make up the two indispensable, undeniable facts of the Gospel of the grace of God. Reminding them of the message he had preached to them, through which message they were saved, he lays upon their hearts the weight of their own responsibility to work earnestly, steadfastly, with a consuming zeal to make known to others the glorious Gospel of the grace of God, the good news of salvation.

Paul's Exhortation to Timothy

"Paul, an apostle of Jesus Christ by the commandment of God our Saviour, and Lord Jesus Christ, which is our hope; unto Timothy, my own son in the faith: Grace, mercy, and peace, from God our Father and Jesus Christ our Lord. As I besought thee to abide still at Ephesus, when I went into Macedonia, that thou mightest charge some that they teach no other doctrine. Neither give heed to fables and endless genealogies, which minister questions, rather than godly edifying which is in faith: so do" (I Tim. 1:1-4).

Here is emphasized Paul's assurance that he is God's minister, delivering the message of God Almighty and the Lord Jesus Christ. In the passage previously quoted from I Timothy 4:11-16 Paul admonished and exhorted his son in the faith to give attendance to reading and to meditation. "Give thyself wholly to them, meditate upon them, *continue* in them."

Beloved, *Christianity is not a part-time responsibility.* There are too many part-time Christians (so called), who give God a few minutes of their time on Sunday morning and take the other six days of the week for themselves. They give God a few pennies on Sunday morning and keep the rest for themselves. Such people are not soul-winners, neither are they spiritually minded; and (assuming that they have ever been saved) they cannot be effective witnesses for Christ.

You will notice, in II Timothy 4:1, Paul gives young Timothy — not a suggestion, but a *divine charge*: "I charge thee therefore *before God, and the Lord Jesus Christ,* who shall judge the quick and the dead at His appearing and His kingdom; PREACH THE WORD!" Any young man who is not willing to face this charge is not fit to be a minister of the Gospel. All Christians should be soul-winners, but this instruction is directed primarily to Timothy in his capacity as a faithful minister of Jesus Christ.

Paul warns this young man of *judgment at Christ's appearing.* When Jesus comes, each believer will be rewarded for his stewardship — and *all faithful stewardship* will receive a reward. I personally believe that the greatest joy of the heart of God is to save the sinner. I further believe that WE, as believers, should strive earnestly and faithfully to get the Gospel message to those who have never heard.

The question has been asked, "Why should *anyone* hear the Gospel twice until *everyone* has heard it *once?*" To young

Timothy Paul said, "Preach the Word — *nothing else!* Be instant at all times — in season, out of season. *Reprove, rebuke, exhort* with all longsuffering and doctrine."

Please notice that reproof and rebuke precede exhortation and doctrine. We need to *reprove and rebuke* the world of sin, and in so doing point out to them their need of a Saviour. We need to *exhort* them to be born again, and then give them *Bible doctrine.*

Paul warned Timothy that the day would come when people would not endure sound doctrine, but would "heap to themselves" (hire) teachers — *and that is the proper word today.* Ministers are "hired" and "fired." There was a time when God *called* preachers and sent them into the field — and this is still true in many instances; but all too often ministers are manufactured in denominational serminaries and turned off the assembly line much as automobile manufacturers turn out automobiles!

The true minister of God is *called* of God, *ordained* of God, and *sent* by God to the assembly over which He appoints that minister His undershepherd.

We are warned that people will turn their ears from the truth and be turned "unto fables." But in spite of the multitudes who will refuse the truth, we are to be faithful in our evangelism. We are to watch (be alert), endure afflictions, make full proof of our ministry. God help us who profess to be ministers to preach the Word of truth — always, under all circumstances and in the face of all difficulties.

Paul's Message to the Galatians

"Paul, an apostle, (not of men, neither by man, but by Jesus Christ, and God the Father, who raised Him from the dead;) And all the brethren which are with me unto the churches of Galatia:

"Grace be unto you and peace from God the Father, and from our Lord Jesus Christ, who gave Himself for our sins, that He might deliver us from the present evil world, according to the will of God and our Father: To whom be the glory for ever and ever. Amen.

"I marvel that ye are so soon removed from Him that called you into the grace of Christ unto another gospel: Which is not another; but there be some that trouble you, and would pervert the Gospel of Christ. *But though we, or an angel from heaven, preach any other gospel unto you than that which we have preached unto you, let him be accursed.* As we said before, so say I now again. *If any man preach any other gospel unto you than that ye have received, let him be accursed.*

"For do I now persuade men, or God? or do I seek to please men? For if I yet pleased men, I should not be the servant of Christ. But I certify you, brethren, that the Gospel which was preached of me is not after man. For I neither received it of man, neither was I taught it, but by the revelation of Jesus Christ. For ye have heard of my conversation in time past in the Jews' religion, how that beyond measure I persecuted the Church of God, and wasted it: and profited in the Jews' religion above many my equals in mine own nation, being more exceedingly zealous of the traditions of my fathers.

"But when it pleased God, who separated me from my mother's womb, and called me by His grace, to reveal His Son in me, that I might preach Him among the heathen; immediately I conferred not with flesh and blood: Neither went I up to Jerusalem to them which were apostles before me; but I went into Arabia, and returned again unto Damascus. Then after three years I went up to Jerusalem to see Peter, and abode with him fifteen days. But other of the apostles saw I none, save James the Lord's brother.

"Now the things which I write unto you, behold, before God, I lie not. Afterwards I came into the regions of Syria and Cilicia; and was unknown by face unto the churches of Judaea which were in Christ: But they had heard only, That he which persecuted us in times past now preacheth the faith which once he destroyed. And they glorified God in me" (Gal. 1:1-24).

As the Apostle Paul writes to the Christians in Galatia, he recalls the great day of his conversion and his amazing experience as he journeyed toward Damascus — the day when his physical eyes were blinded but the eyes of his understanding were opened. With sad and heavy heart he recalled how, "beyond measure," he had persecuted and wasted the Church of the living God. He probably remembered the day Stephen was stoned, seeing that young man's face shine like the face of an angel as he prayed for his executioners, "Lord Jesus, receive my spirit. . . . Lord, lay not this sin to their charge" (Acts 7:54-60).

How amazing to this apostle, that God should call him and that Jesus spoke to him on the Damascus road, when he had persecuted and wasted the Church, allowing believers to be stoned and martyred! But he was thankful. He said, "I thank Christ Jesus our Lord, who hath enabled me, for that He counted me faithful, putting me into the ministry; who was before a blasphemer, and a persecutor, and injurious: but I obtained mercy, because I did it ignorantly in unbelief. And the grace of our Lord was exceeding abundant with faith and love which is in Christ Jesus" (I Tim. 1:12-14).

In I Thessalonians 2:4 he mentions having been "allowed of God to be put *in trust* with the Gospel."

He stresses the truth that the message he preached came to him by revelation direct from God, not by tradition received from other apostles. In other words, Paul said, "I had a revelation from God — a revelation of His crucified, buried, risen Son; and at the same time, He called and ordained me to preach the Gospel of His grace. I was a blasphemer, a persecutor of the Church, who injured many saints — but in spite of it all, He saved me, counted me faithful, and put me in the ministry."

In studying the writings of Paul we see that he was always careful to assure those to whom he ministered that the message he gave was not his, but God's. Over and over again he proclaimed that he was not a minister by choice nor by vocation, but by direct ordination of God Almighty:

"For though I preach the Gospel, I have nothing to glory of: for necessity is laid upon me; yea, woe is unto me, if I preach not the Gospel!" (I Cor. 9:16). His message, therefore, was not his own. It was by revelation from God.

Paul was jealous for the Gospel of the grace of God. According to a passage quoted from our chapter in Galatians, he proclaimed that if anyone — man or angel — should preach any *other* gospel, "let him be accursed" — in other words, *let him drop into hell!*

It would be far better to be a gangster, a dope peddler, a bootlegger, a liar, a thief, a cold-blooded murderer, than to be called a "minister" and pervert the Gospel of the grace of God, delivering to eternal souls a message *other* than that of the grace of God that saves, keeps, and delivers! God have mercy on any person who professes to be a preacher or teacher of the Gospel, and yet perverts the truth of God to please men, to bring glory to himself, to further the cause of a denominational group, or to curry favor with ecclesiastical bosses!

In I Corinthians 9:19, 22 Paul testified, *"For though I be free from all men, yet have I made myself servant unto all, that I might gain the more. . . . I am made all things to all men, that I might by all means save some."*

The same honorable and glorious calling that Paul had is offered to each and every Christian. I do not mean that we can all be apostles, nor that God will call us to pen down thirteen epistles; but we have the privilege of teaching the same glorious Gospel as that preached and taught by Paul!

No one has any priority on the Gospel. You may not be a pastor, an evangelist, or a missionary — but if you are born again you can be a witness for Jesus, giving out the good news that Jesus was crucified, buried, risen, seen of men, ascended into heaven where He is now seated at the right hand of God the Father to make intercession for all who will come unto God by Him!

Who Helped YOU to Find the Way of Salvation?

Jesus saved me — no one but Jesus *could* have saved me, for there is none other name given under heaven among men whereby we must be saved; but *someone helped me to find the WAY to Jesus.* I dare say that you who are born again can remember some one who had a definite part in bringing *you* to the door of salvation and pointing you to Jesus. Perhaps it was your mother, your father, your husband, your wife;

perhaps someone simply handed you a Gospel tract. Perhaps
a pastor, an evangelist, a street preacher put a little salvation
pamphlet in your automobile one day when you parked down-
town. Somewhere, in some way, somebody helped you to find
your way to Jesus!

I definitely know who helped ME — even when I did not
care to BE helped. My mother prayed for me many times,
and I had a sister who was specifically interested in my going
to heaven when seemingly others — myself included — did
not care. They prayed untiringly and would not take "No"
for an answer. They witnessed to me — and I despised them
for doing it. They wrote letters to me — and I read them in
spite of the fact that I did not want to read them. My
sister consistently insisted that I be saved — and because of
her testimony I WAS saved. Therefore, it would be criminal
if I should let others pass by and I refuse or neglect to tell
them about the wonderful Saviour!

But there are so many poor sinner boys and girls who do not
have godly mothers, sisters, fathers, or brothers to pray for
them! If you and I who know Jesus do not pray for them
and witness to them, they will be lost eternally in the lake
of fire. We should say with Paul, "Woe is unto me if I
preach not the Gospel!" May God help us to be willing to do
anything honorable and Christian to help men and women, boys
and girls, to come to the knowledge of Jesus and be saved.

God's Warning

"Son of man, I have made thee a watchman unto the house
of Israel: therefore hear the word at my mouth, and give
them warning from me. When I say unto the wicked, Thou
shalt surely die; and thou givest him not warning, nor speakest
to warn the wicked from his wicked way, to save his life; the
same wicked man shall die in his iniquity; *but his blood will
I require at thine hand.* Yet if thou warn the wicked, and he
turn not from his wickedness, nor from his wicked way, he
shall die in his iniquity; but *thou hast delivered thy soul"*
(Ezek. 3:17-19).

"He which converteth the sinner from the error of his

way shall save a soul from death, and shall hide a multitude of sins" (James 5:20).

Like Paul, we should often remember the day when *we* heard the Gospel and our blinded minds were opened, our hard hearts were melted, our stubborn wills were broken through the hearing of the Word of God — and we yielded our lives to Jesus! We should ask ourselves the question, "What — and where — would we be today had we not heard the Gospel?" No doubt some of us would be in hell by now, others would be steeped in sin, broken in health, hopelessly lost and *on the road* to hell.

Facing this fact, we should give thanks to God for His love and grace, for the shed blood of Jesus, and for the individual or circumstance that pointed us to Christ! God forbid that our sense of indebtedness should ever leave us, or that we should ever look upon the winning of souls as the duty of others — or as something to be done in our spare time when we have nothing *else* to do. May we willingly and determinedly face our responsibility to those who are still blinded, groping in the darkness of sin and shackled by Satan!

The Message That Saves Must Be Positive and Authoritative

Supposition is no good in soul-winning. We who would effectively win souls must, first of all, know for sure that we know the Saviour; we must know for sure that we speak with authority.

Paul could say, ". . . I KNOW whom I have believed, and am persuaded that he is able to keep that which I have committed unto Him against that day" (II Tim. 1:12). Paul knew WHAT he believed, but first and foremost he knew WHOM he believed. He knew a living Christ and he preached a living message:

"And Paul, as his manner was, went in unto them, and three sabbath days reasoned with them out of the Scriptures, opening and alleging, that Christ must needs have suffered, and risen again from the dead; and that this Jesus, whom I preach unto you, is Christ. . . . Then certain philosophers of the Epicureans, and of the Stoicks, encountered him. And some said, What will this babbler say? Other some, He seemeth to be a setter forth of strange gods: because he preached unto them Jesus, and the resurrection" (Acts 17:3, 18).

The secret of Paul's successful ministry was that he always preached "according to the Scriptures." He always declared "Thus saith the Lord." He did not care for human theory or supposition, he did not care for human speculation. He possessed divine revelation, and when he spoke, he spoke with authority. There was no doubt in the mind of the apostle concerning the bodily resurrection of Jesus, and His saving power. He never said, "The way I see it . . . in my humble opinion . . . it may be. . . ." He thundered out the Gospel "according to the Scriptures" — and he spoke with authority, in words easily understood — words that were "the power of God unto salvation" to all who will believe.

The soul-winner must never apologize for preaching the pure, unadulterated Word of God! The man who is not sure that God lives, sure that God loved us and gave Jesus, sure that Jesus died, was buried, rose again and is now seated at the right hand of God, the man who is not sure that *sin is real* and "the wages of sin is death" and equally sure that Christ saves sinners, should never attempt to win souls or preach the Gospel. Believe it or not, beloved, we live in a world that is hungry for a salvation message that is logical, convincing, dogmatic, and authoritative.

We have entirely too many question marks and too much supposition in the pulpits today — too much preaching that is manufactured in denominational seminaries instead of being revealed by the Holy Spirit as the minister searches the Scriptures. The Word of God is the only message that will save a sinner, bring peace to a troubled heart and assurance to a soul on the verge of despair. God help us to sound out this good news to all who need a Saviour.

The Message of Redemption Is the Message of the Cross

A gospel without the cross is not a Gospel. A message void of the shed blood of Jesus is as sounding brass or a tinkling cymbal. The devil does not fear the man in the pulpit or the personal worker who detours around the cross and the blood as the only remission for sin and the only hope for the sinner.

We are living in a day when the masses desire to have their ears tickled with a bloodless gospel devoid of the cross. Paul said to the Corinthians, "For the preaching of the cross is to them that perish foolishness; but unto us which are saved it is the power of God. . . . But we preach Christ crucified, unto the Jews a stumblingblock, and unto the Greeks foolishness; but unto them which are called, both Jews and Greeks, Christ the power of God, and the wisdom of God" (I Cor. 1:8, 23, 24).

"This is a faithful saying, and worthy of all acceptation, that *Christ Jesus came into the world to save sinners . . .*" (I Tim. 1:15). This "faithful saying" is worthy of acceptation because it is time-tested and centuries-proved by those of us who are believers, having received the message by faith. Without the cross, there IS no Gospel, in its true meaning.

The *sinless life* of Jesus could never have saved us. The *miracles* He performed could never have saved us. It was His death on the cruel cross that paid the sin-debt and purchased redemption. So long as He remained upon earth, His sinlessness simply showed ordinary men how exceeding sinful they really were. It was a divine imperative that He go to the cross:

"Except a corn of wheat fall into the ground and die, it abideth alone: but if it die, it bringeth forth much fruit" (John 12:24). Jesus was that corn of wheat. To Nicodemus He said, ". . . As Moses lifted up the serpent in the wilderness, even so *must* the Son of man be lifted up: that whosoever believeth in Him should not perish, but have eternal life" (John 3:14, 15).

A "must" with God is a MUST! There was no other way — it had to be the cross.

There are many new translations of the Bible today. We hear much about bringing it "up to date" to fit the times in which we live. The Bible has *always been* up to date — and will continue to be so. Times change, customs and people change: but *sin* does not change, *Satan* does not change — and neither does the Gospel! The Bible is as up to date as the tick of the watch on your arm, as up to date as tomorrow morning's headlines. Sin is still *sin,* the wages of sin is still *death,* and the Word of God still thunders out: *"Except a man be born again he cannot see the kingdom of God! Except ye repent, ye shall perish!"*

Jesus said, *"And I, if I be lifted up from the earth, will draw all men unto me"* (John 12:32), and the only message that WILL draw men and women out of the gutter of sin and plant their feet on the Solid Rock is the message of the cross, the message of the crucified Saviour and His shed blood. No other message can or will bring salvation.

The Gospel Message Is a Message of Warning

The Apostle Paul preached the death, burial, and resurrection of Jesus Christ. He preached the *love* of God, he preached the *mercy* of God, he preached the *grace* of God — and he did not stop short of preaching the *wrath* of God. He did not preach a chocolate-covered, sugar-coated, easy going, popular message. To the Corinthians he said, *"Knowing the terror of the Lord, we persuade men"* (II Cor. 5:11). That is, "Knowing that God is a God of terror, a God of wrath, we preach *warning,* persuading men to turn to the Lord Jesus Christ lest they fall into the hands of the God of terror."

Hebrews 12:29 tells us, ". . . Our God is a consuming fire." Paul did not preach a one-sided Gospel. He preached the whole counsel of God — the love of God, the wrath of God, the terror of God, and the fire of God's judgment. In his famous sermon on Mars Hill he cried out that God "commandeth all men every where to repent; because He hath appointed a day, in which He will judge the world in righteousness . . ." (Acts 17:30, 31 in part).

Paul believed and preached that it is a divine necessity to repent or perish, but in the modern pulpit we hear very little about repenting, and the old-fashioned mourner's bench has been outlawed. (I realize that mourning and weeping will not save — but those outward emotions do signify a broken and a contrite heart which God will not despise.)

We are saved by trusting Jesus, but we have entirely too few tears of repentance in our churches today, entirely too few invitations for people to repent of their sins and call on God for mercy. Men have met God at an altar down through the centuries, and God has always honored a broken, contrite heart. Godly sorrow worketh repentance, and I do not believe there has ever been an instance of true salvation which was not preceded by godly fear and godly sorrow.

We need more dogmatic, positive preaching concerning the judgment of God, preaching that will cause men to realize the exceeding sinfulness of sin and the drastic need of a Saviour, preaching that will cause men to tremble under the power of the Holy Spirit. We need messages like the Apostle Paul preached to the people in Thessalonica: ". . . The Lord Jesus shall be revealed from heaven with His mighty angels, in flaming fire taking vengeance on them that know not God, and that obey not the Gospel of our Lord Jesus Christ, who shall be punished with everlasting destruction from the presence of the Lord, and from the glory of His power" (II Thess. 1:7-9).

There is no excuse for anyone missing the message here. The Lord Jesus Himself, *in a body*, will one day be revealed. He will be seen coming in the heavens, accompanied by a host of mighty angels and by flaming fire. He will descend from heaven to earth, taking vengeance on those who know not God and who obey not the Gospel. They shall be punished — *not destroyed or annihilated* as some would have us believe — but punished with *everlasting, unending destruction* from the presence of the Lord and from the glory of His power!

We NEED this kind of preaching today. The people need to be informed about the return of Jesus, the coming judgment, the fires of hell, and the eternal damnation of the wicked. In Mark 9:42-48 Jesus Christ preached the hottest sermon ever preached on hell, and He preached it in the plainest, most understandable language.

It is true that the Gospel is good news — the best news any poor sinner could ever hear — and *we must preach the love of God* with the good news of salvation; but we must not stop there. We cannot preach the *grace* of God without also preaching the *judgment* of God. We must tell individuals that if they refuse the Saviour and turn a deaf ear to the call of the Spirit, they will face God as their righteous judge.

Paul said, "IT IS A FEARFUL THING TO FALL INTO THE HANDS OF THE LIVING GOD" (Heb. 10:31) — but it is not *necessary* to fall into the hands of a living God. Right now, this very moment, you can fall into the arms of a loving Saviour! He invites, "Come unto me, and I will give you rest. . . . They that come to me I will in no wise cast out. . . . Whosoever shall call upon the name of the Lord shall be saved. . . . The Spirit and the bride say, Come. Let him that heareth say come. Let him that is thirsty come. *Whosoever will*, let him come!"

That is the invitation of the Lord Jesus to every sinner — but *do it now!* "Boast not thyself of tomorrow, for thou knowest not what a day may bring forth" (Prov. 27:1).

". . . *Now is* the accepted time; behold, *now* is the day of salvation" (II Cor. 6:2).

The Gospel Message Is an Instructive Message

Paul was an evangelist, but he was also a teacher. God *calls* pastors, teachers, evangelists, missionaries — yes; but in one sense we all have the *same* calling. There are different ministries, but all preachers of the Gospel should also be *teachers* of the Gospel, "warning every man, and TEACHING every man in all wisdom; that we may present every man perfect in Christ Jesus" (Col. 1:28).

There are two extremes today — one group believes in extreme (but often superficial) emotionalism. They sing, shout, clap their hands, and have a great meeting where the time is taken up, primarily, by singing, shouting, and hand-clapping. I am not criticizing those who practice this type of emotionalism; I am only pointing out that if we hope to stand in the hour of storm, and if we hope for our converts to weather the storms, we must be sure that they are founded and grounded upon the Solid Rock. Paul never forgot to preach doctrine. He taught his converts Bible doctrine that would give them grace, courage, and strength to stand in the hour of testing.

On the other extreme is the formal crowd who attend services where everything is done by cut-and-dried programming, and the devil knows far in advance what is going to happen, when, and *to whom.* The program is outlined far ahead of time and it cannot be altered, even for the sake of the Holy Spirit. It must go according to schedule — stern orthodoxy, dead religion.

Between these two extremes, then, are the few who preach a dynamic, soul-saving Gospel. They believe in a genuine, heartfelt salvation, and they also teach the Word that will root and ground believers in the faith once delivered to the saints.

Tragedy of Tragedies

In many instances, in far too many churches, those who come forward for church membership do not know a reason for what they are doing. They simply join a church, ask for baptism, and have no knowledge of what it means to believe on the Lord Jesus Christ for salvation. I truly believe that there are many honest seekers of truth and salvation who come foward in a church service and go away with empty hearts and disillusioned minds, without *knowing how* to believe on the Lord Jesus Christ and trust Him to forgive their sins and save their soul. *To me, this is the tragedy of tragedies!*

Perhaps, when these dear souls come forward seeking salvation, the preacher takes their hand, invites them to be seated while the church clerk takes their name and address, and asks them if they are coming into the church by baptism, by letter, or by watch-care. At the close of the invitation hymn he asks them if they believe Jesus Christ to be the Son of God, and they answer, "Yes." They are then "voted into" the church, a baptismal time is set — and no one bothers to open the Word of God to instruct them, no one reads the Scriptures to those who have come forward, no one points out the "why" and the "how" of believing, receiving, and having faith in God.

Thus, the poor souls who came forward with hungry hearts seeking to know Jesus, leave the church as the Ethiopian eunuch left Jerusalem, the city of worship, and was returning home with the same empty hunger in his heart — until Philip met him and expounded unto him the Scriptures.

We must remember that the sinner is dead in trespasses, blinded by sin, bound in the shackles of iniquity, and hopelessly lost! How tragic to hurry through the altar service, bypass the moments of inquiry, and rush an honest seeker of salvation into church membership when he actually has no knowledge of a personal relationship with the Saviour. A large majority of those who come forward are ignorant concerning the Word of God, they have no knowledge of the Gospel; and it is the solemn duty of the Christian to instruct them in the things of God and show them the plan of salvation based on God's Word.

To the Romans Paul said, ". . . Whosoever shall call upon the name of the Lord shall be saved. How then shall they call on Him in whom they have not believed? and how shall they believe in Him of whom they have not heard? and how shall they hear without a preacher? And how shall they preach, except they be sent? As it is written, How beautiful are the feet of them that preach the Gospel of peace and bring glad tidings of good things! But they have not all obeyed the Gospel. For Esaias saith, Lord, who hath believed our report? So then faith cometh by hearing, and hearing by the Word of God" (Rom. 10:13-17).

In these verses Paul gives the plan of salvation in reverse. God calls and sends witnesses who give forth the Word of God — the good news that Jesus Saves. Thus, the Word is heard by the unbeliever, and the Word brings faith. Then faith, born in the heart of the unbeliever through hearing the Word, automatically calls on God and the transaction is complete. Jesus saves the one who calls.

But there can be no saving faith on the part of the seeker of salvation until he first hears the Word of God — not with the ear, but with the heart: "For with the heart man believeth unto righteousness; and with the mouth confession is made unto salvation" (Rom. 10:10). We need to saturate the seeker of salvation with the Word of God.

Jesus said, "Verily, verily, I say unto you, *He that heareth my word,* and believeth on Him that sent me, hath everlasting life, and shall not come into condemnation; but is passed from death unto life" (John 5:24).

I Peter 1:23 says, "Being born again, not of corruptible seed, but of incorruptible, *by the Word of God,* which liveth and abideth for ever."

James said, "Wherefore lay apart all filthiness and superfluity of naughtiness, and receive with meekness *the engrafted Word* which is able to save your souls" (James 1:21).

There can be no salvation, no saving faith, until the unbeliever hears the Word of God.

When the Philippian jailer asked, "What must I do to be saved?" Paul and Silas answered, *"Believe on the Lord Jesus Christ,* and thou shalt be saved, and thy house." But notice: *"And they spake unto him THE WORD OF THE LORD,* and to all that were in his house" (Acts 16:31, 32).

Paul answered the jailer's question. When he asked what he must do to be saved, Paul replied, "Believe on the Lord Jesus Christ" — and that is the ONLY way to be saved. But this poor, blinded, pagan jailer did not know what it *meant* to believe on the Lord Jesus Christ. But Paul knew, and he gave the WORD OF GOD to the jailer and to all of his household. Apart from the Word there is no saving faith, there can be no new birth. It is the *Gospel* that is the power of God unto salvation to those who believe.

But in this atomic age, when men are running to and fro and the whole world is in a frenzy, in most church services the minister gives a short essay or sermonette, folk are invited to unite with the church, and those who desire to do so come forward to give the preacher their name, address, and be voted into the church. The Word of God is not opened, no instruction is given on the meaning of believing on the Lord Jesus Christ unto salvation. Tragedy of tragedies, indeed!

Jesus was a very busy Man, but if you will study the Gospels you will find Him sitting at table with publicans and sinners, instructing and teaching them. You will find Him sitting at Jacob's well, patiently teaching a poor Samaritan woman, leading her to the living water. Our Lord was never too busy, never in too big a hurry, to teach individuals and lead them into the way of salvation.

The natural man cannot know nor understand the things of God until the Holy Spirit comes into his heart. Then He (the Holy Spirit) reveals the things of God. To the believer, God reveals His truth — and it is up to us who believe to teach and preach this truth to unbelievers, to point them to Jesus, and to make the way of salvation clear and plain. When they receive Jesus, they can understand the things of God.

"But God hath revealed them unto us by His Spirit; for the Spirit searcheth all things, yea, the deep things of God. For what man knoweth the things of a man, save the spirit of man which is in him? Even so the things of God knoweth no man, but the Spirit of God. Now we have received, not the spirit of the world, but the spirit which is of God; that we might know the things that are freely given to us of God. Which things also we speak, not in the words which man's wisdom teacheth, but which the Holy Ghost teacheth; comparing spiritual things with spiritual" (I Cor. 2:10-13).

Paul was an evangelist, a missionary, an expositor of the truth. He exhorted, he rebuked, but he also *taught*. To young Timothy he said, "Study to shew thyself approved unto God, a workman that needeth not to be ashamed, rightly dividing the Word of truth" (II Tim. 2:15).

Paul wanted to see men saved — but for every believer he had a still deeper desire to "present every man perfect in Christ Jesus." To the Christians in Corinth he said, "For ye know the grace of our Lord Jesus Christ, that, though He was rich, yet for your sakes He became poor, that ye through His poverty might be rich" (II Cor. 8:9).

In I Corinthians 6:19, 20 he said, "What? Know ye not that your body is the temple of the Holy Ghost which is in you, which ye have of God, and ye are not your own? For ye are bought with a price: therefore glorify God in your body, and in your spirit, which are God's."

Paul was a doctrinal preacher but he had no place in his ministry for dead orthodoxy and cold religious creed. He was dynamic even in his preaching of doctrine. He urged his hearers to live a practical, spiritual life — even in the smallest details of daily living — in their social life, their business affairs, or whatsoever. Christians should live a life that will not bring reproach upon the Saviour.

Paul's Message Was Appealing

The Gospel Paul preached was dogmatic and dynamic, but it was also appealing. He did not take a Gospel club and drive people, but rather, he appealed to them on the grounds of the cross, the blood, and what Jesus had accomplished for them.

He pleaded with the believers in Rome to present their bodies a living sacrifice because of God's mercy and grace, because of God's goodness to them (Rom. 12:1).

He invited the Corinthians to follow him as he followed Christ (I Cor. 4:16). In his second letter to the Corinthians he told them, "Now then we are ambassadors for Christ, as though God did beseech you by us: we pray you in Christ's stead, be ye reconciled to God. . . . We then as workers together with Him, beseech you also that ye receive not the grace of God in vain" (II Cor. 5:20; 6:1).

He said to the believers at Ephesus, "I therefore, the prisoner of the Lord, beseech you that ye walk worthy of the vocation wherewith ye are called, with all lowliness and meekness, with longsuffering, forbearing one another in love; endeavouring to keep the unity of the Spirit in the bond of peace" (Eph. 4:1-3).

As Christians today, we should hear this same pleading message from this Prince of Apostles who counted all things loss that he might be his best for Jesus.

Paul's preaching was not a religious lecture. He delivered a message that sought to lead men to a definite act of faith in God unto salvation, followed by a definite surrender of body, soul, and spirit. True, he was an outstanding theologian, but he was also a down-to-earth evangelist and Bible teacher. God gave him the gift of oratory and the power of appeal, but he always based his message upon the truth of the Gospel. He never added his ideas or suppositions to "thus saith the

Lord." Instead, he challenged, "Let God be true, but every man a liar!" (Rom. 3:4).

Jesus spoke of John the Baptist as "a burning and a shining light." Paul's preaching was characterized by fiery enthusiasm because it came from a heart aglow with total surrender and devotion to Christ. He preached the Word that is "like a fire" (Jer. 23:29).

I believe in a heart-felt salvation and in true emotion; but emotional appeals from the pulpit (the reciting of "sob stories" to move the congregation to tears) without scriptural teaching and Bible doctrine, will produce only superficial results. On the other hand, even *sound theology* that is completely *void* of personal application and warm-hearted appeal can lead only to a Gospel-hardened group of church members. In either case, the result is sad, and should not be.

The pure Gospel of the grace of God, delivered by a man who lives what he preaches, will produce a change in the thinking of the unbeliever who is exposed to such preaching. It will bring a verdict in the heart of the listener. A pure Gospel message delivered from a pure heart will reach the souls of men for Christ, for such a message appeals to the individual and challenges him to do something about the need of his heart. Pure Gospel preaching will create a sense of *need* in the hearts of sinners, along with a sense of fear, a sense of responsibility, a sense of indebtedness — for after all, man is the genius of God's creation, the product of God's creative power.

Pure Gospel preaching carries a message of warning, of wooing, of intreating, urging, pleading and persuading, inviting those who need the Lord to make a definite decision for Christ, receive His finished work, and trust Him as Saviour. Pure Gospel is "the power of God unto salvation to everyone that believeth."

The Gospel Message Is All-Sufficient

The man who preaches the pure Gospel of the grace of God delivers an all-sufficient message. All we need to know about God, the devil, salvation, sin, heaven, hell, and things pertaining to life *here and hereafter* are contained in the Word of God. The Apostle Paul preached with profound conviction that the Gospel is all-sufficient. He believed that the Gospel is the only message to heal the world's ills, heartaches, and woes.

To the Christians in Rome he said, ". . . I am sure that, when I come unto you, I shall come in the fulness of the blessing of the Gospel of Christ" (Rom. 15:29). In Ephesians 3:8 he said, "Unto me, who am less than the least of all saints, is this grace given, that I should preach among the Gentiles the unsearchable riches of Christ."

Paul proclaimed the true Gospel — the message of good news that God so loved that He gave heaven's best, that through His grace sinful man might be brought back into the right relationship with a holy God and find in Him every need for time and for eternity.

His message was not so much what men ought to be and do, but, primarily, what GOD can be in us and through us, and what God has done and will yet do for us and through us in Christ Jesus our Lord and Saviour. Paul laid down the rules of Christian conduct, and yet his message was not a list of negatives. Rather, it was one that sounded out the unsearchable riches of God's grace, inviting men to *receive* that all-sufficient grace and the all-sufficient Saviour in His saving power.

The unbeliever is hopeless, without strength, depraved, and hell-bound — but all who believe on the Lord Jesus Christ and put their trust in His finished work will find every need fully met in Him. In Him we find salvation, victory, and reward!

Paul's Burden

I personally believe that Paul was the most powerful preacher who ever lived, apart from the Lord Jesus Christ. He was clear and logical — in his preaching, in his thinking, in his teaching. His epistles clearly reveal that this man possessed a consuming passion for lost souls. His heart was tender toward those outside of Christ. Of his own brothers in the flesh (Israel) he said, "*I say the truth in Christ, I lie not, my conscience*

*also bearing me witness in the Holy Ghost, that I have great
heaviness and continual sorrow in my heart. For I could wish
that myself were accursed from Christ for my brethren, my
kinsmen according to the flesh"* (Rom. 9:1-3). He carried such
a burden for his own people that he confessed he would be
willing to be accursed from Christ if it would save them!

In Philippians 3:18, 19 he said, ". . . Many walk, of whom
I have told you often, and now tell you even *weeping*, that
they are the enemies of the cross of Christ: Whose end is
destruction, whose God is their belly, and whose glory is in
their shame, who mind earthly things." This great evangelist,
this spiritual giant, could weep over sinners, even though they
were enemies of Christ and would have destroyed even Paul
himself. Not many Christians — ministers, Sunday school
teachers, or laymen — weep over sinners today. We need more
eyes bathed in tears for the sake of winning souls for Christ.

In Galatians 4:19 Paul said, "My little children, of whom
I travail in birth again until Christ be formed in you." He
not only carried a tremendous burden for the lost, but for his
children in the faith as well, that they would go forward and
upward, becoming more like Christ day by day.

Writing to the Corinthian believers he said, "And I will very
gladly spend and be spent for you; though the more abundantly
I love you, the less I be loved" (II Cor. 12:15).

Paul was not ashamed to weep. So great was his passion for
souls, so sharp the pain in his heart because of the fact that
they would spend eternity in hell unless they received the
Gospel message and put their faith in the shed blood of Jesus,
that he compared his agony of soul with the travail of a woman
in childbirth. Yes, Paul could "weep o'er the erring ones."

"He that goeth forth and weepeth, bearing precious seed,
shall doubtless come again with rejoicing, bringing his sheaves,
with him" (Psalm 126:6). Paul was willing to sacrifice anything and everything, he was willing to go to all lengths in
personal sacrifice and loss in order to be instrumental in saving
souls. He hazarded his life time after time. He became ac-
customed to living dangerously. In spite of the trials and per-

secutions which he endured, he bought up every opportunity to witness and point souls to the Saviour.

When he set his face steadfastly toward Jerusalem, he knew that he would be persecuted, he knew he would be arrested. In every city where he had preached he had suffered bonds and afflictions, and he knew that the same treatment awaited him in Jerusalem. Yet he said, "But none of these things move me, neither count I my life dear unto myself, so that I might finish my course with joy, and the ministry, which I have received of the Lord Jesus, to testify the Gospel of the grace of God" (Acts 20:24).

Is this not the need of the Church today? We need ministers and laymen who are willing to go "all out" at any cost to point men and women to the Lamb of God who saves to the uttermost all who will come unto God by Him.

Chapter XI

The Believer and His Hope

"Paul, an apostle of Jesus Christ by the commandment of God our Saviour, and Lord Jesus Christ, which is our hope" (I Tim. 1:1).

"But of the times and the seasons, brethren, ye have no need that I write unto you. For yourselves know perfectly that the day of the Lord so cometh as a thief in the night. For when they shall say, Peace and safety; then sudden destruction cometh upon them, as travail upon a woman with child; and they shall not escape. But ye, brethren, are not in darkness, that that day should overtake you as a thief. Ye are all the children of light, and the children of the day: we are not of the night, nor of darkness. Therefore let us not sleep, as do others; but let us watch and be sober" (I Thess. 5:1-6).

"For the grace of God that bringeth salvation hath appeared to all men, teaching us that, denying ungodliness and worldly lusts, we should live soberly, righteously, and godly, in this present world; Looking for that blessed hope, and the glorious appearing of the great God and our Saviour Jesus Christ; Who gave Himself for us, that He might redeem us from all iniquity, and purify unto Himself a peculiar people, zealous of good works. These things speak, and exhort, and rebuke with all authority. Let no man despise thee" (Tit. 2:11-15).

The second coming of Christ was a theme precious to the heart of Paul. He mentions the second coming of Jesus thirteen times as often as he speaks of baptism. An average of one verse in every chapter of his writings mentions the second coming.

In I Thessalonians 1:9, 10 he said, "For they themselves

shew of us what manner of entering in we had unto you, and how ye turned to God from idols to serve the living and true God; *and to wait for His Son from heaven, whom He raised from the dead, even Jesus, which delivered us from the wrath to come."*

The Thessalonians had heard the Gospel preached, they had turned to God, and in so doing they automatically turned from idols — but they did not stop there. Having turned to the living God, they were created in Christ Jesus unto good works, and they had turned to the living God *to serve.* But that is not all: As they served, they were *waiting for His Son from heaven.*

According to the Gospel revealed to Paul, every born again believer has the *hope* of the coming of Jesus and every recipient of the grace of God *believes* in His second coming.

The grace of God that brings salvation also teaches us to look for "that blessed hope" — and if you, dear reader, do not believe in the second coming of Jesus Christ, if you do not expect Him to return to this earth, that is a sure sign that your experience is not authentic and your supposed-to-be conversion was only counterfeit!

Redemption is instantaneous, and the moment we are redeemed we are just as thoroughly and completely redeemed as we will ever be; but salvation is continuous from the moment we are redeemed until we are glorified. We are to "work out our own salvation with fear and trembling." We are to grow in grace and in the knowledge of our Lord and Saviour, Jesus Christ.

In Romans 5:1, 2 Paul clearly teaches that we are justified by faith — but notice: We have *justification,* then *peace,* then *access,* then *grace, joy, hope,* and lastly — *glory!* Salvation is justification through faith; and we will be glorified when Jesus comes in the Rapture and the first resurrection.

In Romans 8:14-17 we read that we are the sons of God (v. 14), we are *adopted* (v. 15), we have *assurance* (v. 16), we are *heirs of God* and joint-heirs with Christ (v. 17). The Scriptures clearly teach that the Christian experience is progressive. Until we see Jesus and receive a glorified body, there is no height in the Christian life which offers no further ground for ascension. Every height attained by the believer puts him in position to reach still *higher* ground in his Christian experience. He never reaches the place where he can settle down with the thought in mind that he has reached the pinnacle of God's grace and there is nothing more to be attained.

As Paul sat in a Roman prison, he wrote to the church at Philippi:

"Not as though I had already attained, either were already perfect: but I follow after, if that I may apprehend that for which also I am apprehended of Christ Jesus. Brethren, I count not myself to have apprehended: but this one thing I do, forgetting those things which are behind, and reaching forth unto those things which are before, I press toward the mark for the prize of the high calling of God in Christ Jesus. . . . For our conversation [citizenship] is in heaven: from whence also we look for the Saviour, the Lord Jesus Christ: Who shall change our vile body, that it may be fashioned like unto His glorious body, according to the working whereby He is able even to subdue all things unto Himself" (Phil. 3:12-21 in part).

The believer who is perfectly satisfied and "at ease in Zion" should visit the altar and repent, for he is on the verge of backsliding — if not already in a backslidden condition! Eternal life is always reaching out, pressing on, looking toward new horizons, probing new depths in the unsearchable riches of God's grace. Present blessings do not suffice for the blessings that can be ours in abundant life. Present truth, glorious as it is, does not blind us to truth that can be sought in the Word of God, truth that is far beyond man's finite mind. The believer who is content to remain as he *is* is on dangerous ground.

Salvation begins in grace, continues in godliness, and climaxes in glory! When we exercise faith in the finished work of the Lord Jesus and His shed blood, our sins are forgiven, we are justified by His blood, we are adopted as God's very own, and *we will be glorified* when we see Jesus as He is!

The Hope of the Believer Is Sure

"But I would not have you to be ignorant, brethren, concerning them which are asleep, that ye sorrow not, even as others which have no hope. For if we believe that Jesus died and rose again, even so them also which sleep in Jesus will God bring with Him. For this we say unto you by the Word of The Lord, that we which are alive and remain unto the coming of the Lord shall not prevent them which are asleep. For the Lord Himself shall descend from heaven with a shout, with the voice of the archangel, and with the trump of God: and the dead in Christ shall rise first: Then we which are alive and remain shall be caught up together with them in the clouds, to meet the Lord in the air: and so shall we ever be with the Lord. Wherefore comfort one another with these words" (I Thess. 4:13-18).

If the Thessalonian Christians entertained any doubt concerning the second coming of Christ, Paul wanted that doubt removed. *"I would not have you to be ignorant,"* he said. He wanted them to know from whom he *received* his message: "This we say unto you BY THE WORD OF THE LORD." He declares Divine authority for the statements made concerning the return of the Lord — yes, even His personal, *bodily* return: "The Lord HIMSELF shall descend from heaven with a shout." There is no fact in Scripture more clearly stated and permanently settled than the fact of the second coming of Jesus. This is the hope of the believer — the hope of all creation (Rom. 8:22, 23).

In Acts 1:8, 9 Jesus instructed the disciples to remain in Jerusalem until they were endued with power from on high: ". . . Ye shall receive power, after that the Holy Ghost is come upon you: and ye shall be witnesses unto me both in Jerusalem, and in all Judaea, and in Samaria, and unto the uttermost part of the earth. And when He had spoken these things, while they beheld, He was taken up; and a cloud received Him out of their sight."

Notice: *"While they beheld. . . ."* They were looking directly at Him, and as they gazed upon Him He was taken up and a cloud received Him out of their sight. And even while they still gazed up into the heavens, two messengers stood by them:

"And while they looked stedfastly toward heaven as He went up, behold, two men stood by them in white apparel; which also said, Ye men of Galilee, why stand ye gazing up into heaven? *This same Jesus, which is taken up from you into heaven, shall so come in like manner as ye have seen Him go into heaven'* " (Acts 1:10, 11).

This SAME JESUS — not a spirit, not an angel, not a cherub, not a saint, but *the same Jesus whom they had known,* with whom they had walked, whom they had touched — Jesus in a body — would come again *in the same manner* as they saw Him go into heaven. There can be no doubt about that statement; it is clear, concise — and divinely settled. In spite of what the liberals, the modernists, or anyone else may say about it, Jesus Christ is coming back to this earth *personally* — and His return (first *for* the Church and then *with* the Church) is the hope of not only the Church, but of *all creation.*

In John 14:1-3 Jesus comforted His disciples with these words: "Let not your heart be troubled: Ye believe in God, believe also in me. In my Father's house are many mansions: if it were not so, I would have told you. I go to prepare a place for you. And if I go and prepare a place for you, I will come again, and receive you unto myself; that where I am, there ye may be also."

Jesus did not tell His saddened disciples that He would send the Holy Spirit for them, or that He would send an angel, or some other representative from heaven. He said, "I am going away, I will prepare a place for you, and I WILL COME AGAIN" — and He will do exactly what He *said* He would do.

Not All Believers Will Die

Many believers will cheat the grave, for when Jesus comes for the Church there will be many believers *living* — and in a moment, "in the twinkling of an eye," these will be changed, and together with those who are raised incorruptible they will be caught up in the clouds to meet the Lord in the air:

"Behold, I shew you a mystery: We shall not all sleep, but we shall all be changed, in a moment, in the twinkling of an eye, at the last trump: For the trumpet shall sound, and the dead shall be raised incorruptible, and we shall be changed. For this corruptible must put on incorruption, and this mortal must put on immortality. So when this corruptible shall have put on incorruption, and this mortal shall have put on immortality, then shall be brought to pass the saying that is written, *Death is swallowed up in victory!*" (I Cor. 15:51-54).

The coming of Jesus in the Rapture will be unannounced. He will come as a thief in the night, He will gather His jewels, and they will be caught up to meet Him in the air. When He comes in the Rapture, He will not stand upon the earth, but when He comes with the Church at the end of the Tribulation, He WILL stand on the Mount of Olives (Zech. 14:4). He will first come FOR the Church, and later He will come WITH the Church. This is the blessed hope, the glorious event, that lies ahead for the Christian.

Paul did not abandon his hope in the return of the Lord, even though his earthly sojourn was drawing to a close. He declared, ". . . I am now ready to be offered, and the time of my departure is at hand. I have fought a good fight, I have finished my course, I have kept the faith: *Henceforth there is laid up for me a crown of righteousness, which the Lord, the righteous Judge, shall give me at that day; and not to me only, but unto all them also that love His appearing*" (II Tim. 4:6-8).

Even though this blessed promise is clearly stated in the Word of God, there are ministers in pulpits across this great land, this country known as "Christian America," who never mention the second coming of Jesus Christ! Satan despises the preaching of the second coming — that blessed, happy, purifying hope; and he therefore puts men in the pulpit who take up the ministry as a vocation instead of a holy calling, and they preach a social Gospel, explaining away these tremendous truths by spiritualizing them. They say, "Christ is *continually* coming as souls are saved" — and this is true in a sense; but certainly *"this same Jesus"* does not come when a sinner is saved — not in like manner as He was seen to go into heaven! Therefore, the conversion of a sinner is not the second coming (the return) of the Lord.

Pentecost was not the return of the Lord, nor is His return when a believer departs this life and goes to be with Him. Christ is coming back to this earth exactly as He went away — He is coming back *bodily, in person.*

Will the Church Convert the World?

There are those who teach that the second coming of Christ means the gradual spread of the Gospel, by which process the world will eventually be converted. This, they say, will come about by a slow but sure Christianization of all nations when they accept the principles of Christ's kingdom; and then His kingdom of peace and brotherhood will be established here upon this earth.

To teach that the Church will convert the world is to display inexcusable scriptural ignorance! There is no place in all of the Word of God where such an idea is even suggested or intimated. The second coming of Christ (according to His own words) will be "as the lightning cometh out of the east, and shineth even unto the west" (Matt. 24:27). It will be instantaneous, and it will be over in a moment. It will be unexpected — it will not be a gradual process through time, But "in the twinkling of an eye," in a split second!

Contrary to some of the erroneous teaching abroad in the land, the world will NOT become better before Jesus comes. Scripture teaches quite the opposite:

"Knowing this first, that there shall come in the last days scoffers, walking after their own lusts, and saying, Where is the promise of His coming? For since the fathers fell asleep, all things continue as they were from the beginning of the creation. For this they willingly are ignorant of, that by the Word of God the heavens were of old, and the earth standing out of the water and in the water: Whereby the world that then was, being overflowed with water, perished: But the heavens and the earth, which are now, by the same word are kept in store, reserved unto fire against the day of judgment and perdition of ungodly men.

But, beloved, be not ignorant of this one thing, that one day is with the Lord as a thousand years, and a thousand years as one day. The Lord is not slack concerning His promise, as some men count slackness; but is longsuffering to us-ward, not willing that any should perish, but that all should come to repentance. But the day of the Lord will come as a thief in the night; in the which the heavens shall pass away with a great noise, and the elements shall melt with fervent heat, the earth also and the works that are therein shall be burned up. Seeing then that all these things shall be dissolved, what manner of persons ought ye to be in all holy conversation and godliness, looking for and hasting unto the coming of the day of God, wherein the heavens being on fire shall be dissolved, and the elements shall melt with fervent heat?" (II Pet. 3:3-12).

Certainly this does not sound like the Church will convert the world, nor that the Gospel will finally bring all men to Christ. The Church was not put here to convert the world, but to call out disciples. Jesus taught that He would return to this earth at a time when gross sinfulness would abound and a state of *deterioration*, not righteousness, would prevail. The Apostle Paul preached the same truth:

"Now the Spirit speaketh expressly, that in the latter times some shall depart from the faith, giving heed to seducing spirits, and doctrines of devils; speaking lies in hypocrisy; having their conscience seared with a hot iron" (I Tim. 4:1, 2).

"This know also, that in the last days perilous times shall come. For men shall be lovers of their own selves, covetous, boasters, proud, blasphemers, disobedient to parents, unthankful, unholy, without natural affection, trucebreakers, false accusers, incontinent, fierce, despisers of those that are good, traitors, heady, highminded, lovers of pleasures more than lovers of God; having a form of godliness, but denying the power thereof: from such turn away.

"For of this sort are they which creep into houses, and lead captive silly women laden with sins, led away with divers lusts, ever learning, and never able to come to the knowledge of the truth. Now as Jannes and Jambres withstood Moses, so do these also resist the truth: men of corrupt minds, reprobate concerning the faith . . . but evil men and seducers shall wax worse and worse, deceiving and being deceived" (II Tim. 3:1-13 in part).

These impressive truths from God's Word do not suggest that the world will become better and better until it is finally fully converted to Christianity. O, no! Rather, they teach that men will become worse and worse, iniquity will abound, ungodliness will spread like a flood — and Jesus will come in the darkest hour of human history!

Dispensational Truth

The Bible is a book of dispensational truth, and when men refuse to face this fact it is impossible for them to understand the Scriptures — especially those relative to the second coming. Paul commands, "Study to shew thyself approved unto God, a workman that needeth not to be ashamed, *rightly dividing the Word of truth*" (II Tim. 2:15) — but there are those who refuse to study and others who refuse rightly to divide the Word.

The only way to understand the Bible is to compare Scripture with Scripture, and spiritual things with spiritual. There are *seven dispensations* set forth in the Word of God:

1. The Dispensation of Innocence, which ended in Genesis 2:25.
2. The Dispensation of Conscience — Genesis 3:23 — Genesis 8:20.
3. The Dispensation of Human Government — Genesis 8:20 — Genesis 11:9.
4. The Dispensation of Promise — Genesis 12:1 — Exodus 19:7.
5. The Dispensation of Law — Exodus 19:8 — Matthew 27:35.
6. This present Dispensation of Grace — John 1:17 until the Rapture of the Church. (After the Rapture the Antichrist will reign on the earth for approximately seven years and at the end of His reign Jesus will return with the Church to set up the Kingdom.)

7. The Dispensation of the Kingdom (the Millennium age) — Ephesians 1:10; I Corinthians 15:23-25; Revelation 20:1-6.

It is nothing short of spiritual robbery to take the promises God made to Abraham and to the Kingdom Age, and give those promises to the Church. The Kingdom and the Church are *not* one and the same. We are given a clear outline of God's doings at this particular time, and of what He will do until the setting up of the Kingdom on earth:

"And after they had held their peace, James answered, saying, Men and brethren, hearken unto me: Simeon hath declared how God at the first did visit the Gentiles, to take out of them a people for His name. And to this agree the words of the prophets; as it is written, After this I will return, and will build again the tabernacle of David, which is fallen down; and I will build again the ruins thereof, and I will set it up: That the residue of men might seek after the Lord, and all the Gentiles, upon whom my name is called, saith the Lord, who doeth all these things. *Known unto God are all His works from the beginning of the world* (Acts 15:13-18).

Here it is clearly stated that God would first visit the Gentiles to take out of them a people for His name — and to this, all the prophets agree.

After the Church is caught out, Jesus will return and build again the tabernacle of David. That will take place after the reign of Antichrist. Jesus will sit on the throne of David in the tabernacle of David, and will reign here on this earth for one thousand glorious years!

In the annunciation (Luke 1:26-38) the angel Gabriel said to Mary, ". . . Behold, thou shalt conceive in thy womb, and bring forth a Son, and shalt call His name JESUS. He shall be great, and shall be called the Son of the Highest: *and the Lord God shall give unto Him the throne of His father David: And He shall reign over the house of Jacob for ever; and of His kingdom there shall be no end!*"

The throne of David is a historical fact just as surely as the throne of Caesar is a historical fact — and Jesus will sit on that throne one day, in Jerusalem, to reign over the entire earth. At that time, there will be "peace on earth, good will toward men." Swords will be turned into plowshares, spears into pruning hooks, and men will study war no more. The knowledge of the Lord will cover the earth, the peace that we hear so much about will then be a reality — when the Prince of Peace sits on the throne of David in Jerusalem.

According to God's timeclock of prophecy, the next great event in store for this old world is the Rapture of the Church. Every born again, blood washed believer will be taken out of this earth, caught up to meet Jesus in the air. There will be not one Christian left upon the earth, not one born again person. Antichrist will come, and while he will be accepted by the masses, there will be a sealed remnant of Israel who will preach the Gospel of the Kingdom to those who have never heard the Gospel of Grace. A great multitude will be saved during the reign of the Antichrist, through the preaching of the 144,000 missionaries.

But those who are saved during that time will forfeit their lives. They will be murdered, butchered, they will suffer miseries untold. So fierce will be the persecution that Jesus said of it, "Except those days should be shortened, there should no flesh be saved: but for the elect's sake those days shall be shortened" (Matt. 24:22).

Jesus will return to the earth, and will destroy the armies of Antichrist. Satan will be put in the lake of fire and sealed there for one thousand years, during which there will be a time of glorious peace on earth.

I repeat, the Church was not put here to convert the world nor to bring in the Kingdom. There can BE no kingdom without a king, and the Kingdom will be set up when the King returns.

The Church is here to witness and to preach the Gospel through which individuals are called into the body of Christ; and when that body is complete, Jesus will come for the Church and we will be caught out of this earth to meet Him in the clouds in the air.

The second coming of Christ is clear to all who will believe the Scriptures and allow God to be true and every man a liar. There need be no confusion on the subject for those who will read the New Testament with an open heart and an open mind, forgetting religious dogma, doctrine, and traditions of men, and let the Word of God speak.

For 1900 years now, as the Gospel of the grace of God is preached by believers, souls are called by the Holy Spirit — and when they hear and receive the Word, they become members of the spiritual body of Christ, the New Testament Church. This will continue until the Church is complete.. Jesus will then return and catch away the Church, reward believers for their stewardship, and at the end of the reign of Antichrist we will return to reign with Christ right here upon the earth for one thousand glorious years of peace.

For the Christian, the best is just ahead — *the blessed hope, the glorious appearing of the great God and our Saviour Jesus Christ,* who loved us and gave Himself to redeem us. We are predestined to be conformed to His image, and when we see Him we will be like Him (I John 3:1-3).

The Return of Jesus Our Hope

The hope of the believer, the hope of our departed loved ones, the hope of the Church, the hope of *all creation,* is the return of the Lord. Paul admonished the Thessalonian believers, "Wherefore comfort one another with these words" (I Thess. 4:18).

In II Thessalonians 2:14-17 in part, he said, "Whereunto He called you by our Gospel, to the obtaining of the glory of our Lord Jesus Christ. . . . Now our Lord Jesus Christ Himself, and God, even our Father, which hath loved us, and hath given us everlasting consolation and good hope through grace, comfort your hearts, and stablish you in every good word and work."

In I Thessalonians 5:11 we read, "Wherefore comfort yourselves together, and edify one another, even as also ye do."

In I Corinthians 14:3 Paul said, ". . . He that prophesieth speaketh unto men to edification, and exhortation, and comfort."

In all of God's Word there is no other message that brings such comfort to the heart of the believer as does the message of the soon coming of Jesus Christ! It is so wonderful to know, in these dark and trying days, that at any moment of any hour, Jesus can come. The signs of the times are all around us. The night is far spent, the day is at hand. Evil men and seducers ARE waxing

worse and worse. Iniquity is abounding on every hand. Men
are lovers of pleasure more than lovers of God. The fig tree is
budding and putting forth tender leaves. Beloved, spiritually
minded believers are listening for the shout that will call us to
higher ground!

What Will Actually Take Place When Jesus Comes in the Rapture?

The Word of God clearly states that Jesus will come "as a
thief in the night." The same Bible states that He will come
"and every eye shall see Him." But there is no contradiction
here:

The coming that is likened unto a thief in the night is the
Rapture, when Jesus comes for His Church. This is the coming
as spoken of in I Thessalonians 5 and II Peter 3.

Every eye shall see Him when He comes in the *Revelation,*
"in flaming fire taking vengeance on them that know not God,
and that obey not the Gospel of our Lord Jesus Christ" (II Thess.
1:8).

What will actually take place when Jesus comes in the
Rapture? First, according to I Thessalonians 4:13-18, Jesus will
descend from heaven into the atmosphere just above the earth.
The trumpet will sound, and the bodies of believers who have
departed this life will be raised. The spirits of these believers
will be with Jesus, He will bring them with Him when He comes,
and the spirit will be united with the resurrected, glorified body.

Then, believers who are living when Jesus comes will be
changed "in a moment," and together we will be caught up into
the clouds in the air to meet Him:

"Behold, I shew you a mystery: We shall not all sleep, but we
shall all be changed. In a moment, in the twinkling of an eye, at
the last trump: For the trumpet shall sound, and the dead shall
be raised incorruptible, and we shall be changed. For this corruptible must put on incorruption, and this mortal must put on
immortality" (I Cor. 15:51-53).

Paul declares that the resurrection of the body is definitely
part of the hope of the believer, and in the tremendous fifteenth
chapter of I Corinthians he gives no less than fifty-seven verses

on that subject. He clearly states that the believer's resurrection body will be incorruptible (v. 42), it will be a glorious, powerful body (v. 43), it will be a spiritual body (v. 44), it will be a heavenly body (vv. 48, 49).

For the saints who are living when Jesus comes in the Rapture, the corruptible will instantaneously put on incorruption, and we will have the same glorious, powerful, spiritual, heavenly body as the resurrection body of Jesus.

Paul declared this to be a mystery, but no less a fact. We will not all die — some of us will cheat the grave; but we will all be changed, we will all possess a glorified body. We are waiting for that redemption(Rom. 8:23; Eph. 1:14).

Oh, yes — there are skeptics (Paul called them "fools"), who ask, "How are the dead raised up? And with what body do they come?" He replied, "Thou fool, that which thou sowest is not quickened, except it die: And that which thou sowest, thou sowest not that body that shall be, but bare grain, it may chance of wheat, or of some other grain: *But God giveth it a body as it hath pleased Him, and to every seed his own body*" (I Cor. 15:35-38).

If God is able to give every little grain its own individual body, He is most assuredly able to give *man* a glorified body as it pleases Him. This may be a mystery to us, but it is not a mystery to the God of all creation. Man was created in God's image, and our glorified bodies will bear the image of His glorious body: ". . . As we have borne the image of the earthy, we shall also bear the image of the heavenly" (I Cor. 15:49).

Not only will we receive a glorified body, but we will be united with our loved ones and friends who have gone on before us. Practically every one of us can say, "I have a loved one in Paradise, resting with Jesus."

"And I heard a voice from heaven saying unto me, Write, *Blessed are the dead which die in the Lord from henceforth: Yea, saith the Spirit, that they may rest from their labours; and their works do follow them*" (Rev. 14:13).

To be absent from the body is to be present with the Lord (II Cor. 5:8). We know our saved and departed loved ones are with Jesus now, we know they are conscious, and they are happy; but we will never be reunited with them until the Rapture and the first resurrection. There is no time element between the departure of this life and the entering with Jesus (Luke 23:43). Unconsciousness of the dead (popularly known as "soul-sleep") is a doctrine of demons, not of the Word of God.

Many ask, "Will we know our loved ones in heaven?" Indeed we shall! Now we know "in part," but then shall we know "even as we are known." On the Mount of Transfiguration, when Moses and Elijah came down and met with Jesus, Peter, James, and John recognized them even though Moses and Elijah had departed this life centuries before. We will have glorified bodies, but we will know as we are known and our glorified body will resemble our earthly body, but it will be free from sin, pain, imperfection, and corruption.

Yes, mother — you will know your child in heaven. Wife, you will know your husband. Father, you will know your children. We will know our friends, neighbors, and loved ones, for we will have the mind of Christ. There will be no strangers in that Pearly White City — we will know everyone, we will all be brothers and sisters. We will live next door to Jesus. The light of His face will illumine the city, and we will live in the light of it.

Believers Will Be Rewarded for Their Stewardship

There are those who teach and preach that all believers will share and share alike in rewards, but this teaching is contrary to truth. According to the Word of God, each and every individual will receive his own reward:

"For we must all appear before the judgment seat of Christ; that every one may receive the things done in his body, according to that he hath done, whether it be good or bad" (II Cor. 5:10).

"For other foundation can no man lay than that is laid, which is Jesus Christ. Now if any man build upon this foundation gold, silver, precious stones, wood, hay, stubble; every man's work shall be made manifest: for the day shall declare it, because it shall be revealed by fire; and the fire shall try every man's work of what sort it is. *If any man's work abide which he hath built thereupon, he shall receive a reward. If any man's work shall be burned, he shall suffer loss*: but he himself shall be saved; yet so as by fire" (I Cor. 3:11-15).

The judgment seat of Christ is expressly for believers. It has nothing to do with whether one is saved or lost, but with *rewards*.

The Great White Throne judgment mentioned in Revelation 20:11 has to do with the unsaved. No believer will be judged at the Great White Throne; only the wicked will be there. At that time *the righteous will sit with Jesus* as He judges.

Let us analyze the passage just quoted from I Corinthians:

First, there is *one foundation,* the foundation is already laid, and that foundation is Jesus Christ.

Men build upon that foundation with two types of material: (1) Gold, silver, precious stones; (2) wood, hay, stubble.

We notice that every man's work, the work of each individual, shall be brought to light and displayed.

". . . The day shall declare it. . . . it shall be revealed by fire." *"The day"* referred to here is the judgment day for believers. Jeremiah 23:29 declares that *God's Word* is like fire. So we know that our stewardship will be judged according to the Word of the living God.

Notice that the fire shall try the work of each individual *"of what SORT it is,"* not how *much.* God does not reward according to the bigness or greatness, but according to the quality of our work and the sincerity and purpose behind it. If what we do is done to the glory of God, even if it be but a cup of cold water given in the name of Jesus, it will be rewarded. But if what we do, regardless of how oustanding it may be, is done to be seen of men or to bring glory to ourselves, our stewardship is worthless and will be burned. It is the *sort* of stewardship, not the amount, that counts with God.

If an individual's work stands the fire test, that man will be rewarded; but if his work does not stand the test and is burned, he shall suffer loss — loss of *reward,* not loss of his soul. This deals with stewardship, not with salvation. The man will suffer loss of reward *"but he himself shall be saved; YET SO AS BY FIRE."* His spirit will be saved, but his life's labors will be lost.

What it will be like to be in heaven without reward, I do not

know; but if we believe the Word of God and face this plain
Scripture, we know that there *will be* believers there without a
reward. How sad that will be! Beloved, I want some trophies to
lay at His feet, I want some crowns to lay before Him when we
crown Him Lord of all! Don't you?

(Incidentally, there is no Scripture to suggest that we will
put on our crowns and parade all over God's heaven. Oh, no!
we will not wear our crowns. We will crown HIM Lord of all,
and we will cast our crowns at His feet, for He is worthy!)

In John 15:1-8 Jesus said to His disciples, "I am the true vine,
and my Father is the husbandman. Every branch in me that
beareth not fruit He taketh away: and every branch that beareth
fruit, He purgeth it, that it may bring forth more fruit. Now ye
are clean through the Word which I have spoken unto you.
Abide in me, and I in you. As the branch cannot bear fruit of
itself, except it abide in the vine; no more can ye, except ye
abide in me. I am the vine, ye are the branches: He that
abideth in me, and I in him, the same bringeth forth much
fruit: for without me ye can do nothing. If a man abide not in
me, he is cast forth as a branch, and is withered; and men gather
them, and cast them into the fire, and they are burned. If ye
abide in me, and my words abide in you, ye shall ask what ye
will, and it shall be done unto you. Herein is my Father glorified, that ye bear much fruit; so shall ye be my disciples."

It should humble our hearts to know that we are connected to
the true Vine — and dearly beloved, the *trunk* of the vine does
not bear the fruit: the *branches* bear the fruit. So you see, God
has greatly honored us in allowing us to be branches connected
to the true Vine, Jesus, that we may bear fruit for Him.

Every branch that bears fruit is purged, that it may bring
forth MORE fruit. And "He that abideth in me, and I in him,
the same bringeth forth MUCH fruit." He who allows Jesus to
have full sway in his life brings forth *"much fruit,"* and *God is
glorified when we bring forth much fruit.*

Do you desire to glorify God the Father, He who loved us so
much that He gave His only begotten Son to die for us? There
is only one way to bear "much fruit," and that is to be completely
yielded to the Lord — soul, spirit, and body. He has chosen us

and ordained us to bring forth fruit. May God help us to be fruit-bearing Christians, even to a hundredfold — not just to receive a reward, but to glorify God the Father who provided salvation for us!

John the Beloved gives some important and interesting facts concerning *"full* rewards." In II John 7-11 we read, "For many deceivers are entered into the world, who confess not that Jesus Christ is come in the flesh. This is a deceiver and an antichrist. *Look to yourselves, that we lose not those things which we have wrought, but that we receive a full reward.* Whosoever transgresseth, and abideth not in the doctrine of Christ, hath not God. He that abideth in the doctrine of Christ, he hath both the Father and the Son. *If there come any unto you, and bring not this doctrine, receive him not into your house, neither bid him God speed: For he that biddeth him God speed is partaker of his evil deeds!"*

The solemn warning is simply this: If we support (bid God speed to) the false teachers and false preachers who deviate from the Gospel of grace, we will not receive a FULL REWARD. John warns, "Watch yourself, be careful, that we lose not those things which we have WROUGHT." This has nothing to do with redemption, we do not redeem ourselves, our redemption is not *"wrought"* by us — but stewardship IS; and we must be careful that we lose not our reward for stewardship.

It is certainly scriptural to warn that believers may lose part (or all) of their reward, being saved "so as by fire." I do not want this to happen to me, and I am sure you do not want it to happen to YOU. So let us put on the whole armor of God, abide in Jesus and allow His Word to abide in us, and pray that God will help us to be fruit-bearing believers, to His glory.

It is no wonder that Paul calls the second coming *"the glorious appearing!"* We will receive our glorified bodies, we will be reunited with our departed loved ones, we will be rewarded for our faithful stewardship, we will sit with Jesus at the marriage supper in the sky, and then return to reign with Him on this earth for one thousand glorious years!

Jesus said, "In the world ye shall have tribulation: *but be of good cheer; I HAVE OVERCOME THE WORLD*" (John 16: 33).

". . . Weeping may endure for a night, but joy cometh in the morning" (Psa. 30:5).

We can sincerely join John the Beloved in this prayer: "Even so, COME, Lord Jesus!"

The imminent return of Jesus should cause every unbeliever to stop, think — and *repent!* Jesus said, "Of that day and hour knoweth no man, no, not the angels of heaven, but my Father only" (Matt. 24:36). It may be today. It *could be* this hour. And in the light of that fact, *UNSAVED FRIEND, HEAR THESE WORDS* that fell from the lips of the Lord Jesus:

". . . Then shall appear the sign of the Son of man in heaven: and then shall all the tribes of the earth mourn, and they shall see the Son of man coming in the clouds of heaven with power and great glory" (Matt. 24:30).

". . . If thy hand offend thee, cut it off: it is better for thee to enter into life maimed, than having two hands to go into hell, into the fire that never shall be quenched: Where their worm dieth not, and the fire is not quenched. And if thy foot offend thee, cut it off: It is better for thee to enter halt into life, than having two feet to be cast into hell, into the fire that never shall be quenched: Where their worm dieth not, and the fire is not quenched. And if thine eye offend thee, pluck it out: It is better for thee to enter into the kingdom of God with one eye, than having two eyes to be cast into hell fire: Where their worm dieth not, and the fire is not quenched" (Mark 9:43-48).

"Marvel not at this: for the hour is coming, in the which all that are in the graves shall hear His voice, and shall come forth; they that have done good, unto the resurrection of life; and they that have done evil, unto the resurrection of damnation" (John 2:28, 29).

Now hear these words penned by the minister to the Gentiles, the apostle to the Church:

"*Be not deceived; God is not mocked: For whatsoever a man soweth, that shall he also reap. For he that soweth to his flesh shall of the flesh reap corruption; but he that soweth to the Spirit shall of the Spirit reap life everlasting*" (Gal. 6:7, 8).

In the light of these clear truths laid down in the Word of God, knowing that the wages of sin is death and that judgment is just ahead, knowing that eternal destruction awaits the wicked, is it unreasonable to call every sinner to repentance? There IS no other way of escape. Jesus said, *"Except ye repent, ye shall all likewise perish!"* (Luke 13:3, 5).

Without repentance there is no salvation. It is appointed unto man once to die, and after death, the judgment. It is a Bible fact that Jesus is coming, and it could be this hour. If you are an unbeliever, this is the day, this is the hour, this is the moment when you should repent and call on God; for He has appointed a day when you will be judged in righteousness, and you will receive from the hand of Almighty God exactly what is coming to you! The only way to escape the damnation of hell is to believe on the Lord Jesus Christ and repent of your sins. If you have not done it, *do it now!*

The imminent coming of Christ in the Rapture should challenge us as Christians to search our hearts and allow God to turn the light of His Word and the Holy Spirit upon our souls, lest there be anything that would hinder our being the kind of witness we *should* be for Jesus in this dark world. The grace of God that brings salvation teaches us to deny worldly lusts, to live a sober, godly, righteous life right here in this present world, always looking for that blessed hope and the glorious appearing of the great God and our Saviour Jesus Christ, occupying until He comes.

I wonder if we are living as we would like to be living if Jesus should come this very moment? I wonder if we are looking for His return as expectantly as we would like to be should He return this very moment?

The person who is looking for Jesus will be clean, consecrated, dedicated: "EVERY MAN THAT HATH THIS HOPE IN HIM PURIFIETH HIMSELF, EVEN AS HE IS PURE" (I John 3:3). When the fact of Christ's coming grips us, heart and soul, we will cease to compromise with sin and with the enemies of Jesus. There is no truth in all of the Word of God that will cause Christians to be so spiritually minded and dedicated as will the truth of the imminent return of Jesus to this earth.

Knowing that He is coming at any moment, seeing our friends and sometimes our own loved ones lost and bound for hell, the fact of His imminent return should lay upon us a deep burden to rescue those who are lost. His soon return should cause us to look on the fields that are white unto harvest, and become reapers, not star-gazers. Night is far spent, the day is at hand, and we should be about the Father's business — the business of rescuing the perishing:

"Therefore, my beloved brethren, be ye stedfast, unmoveable, always abounding in the work of the Lord, forasmuch as ye know that your labour is not in vain in the Lord" (I Cor. 15:58).

The time left for soul-winning is limited. It *cannot* be long until Jesus returns. We do not know how soon He will come, but we DO know that He is coming.

It is one thing to be occupied with His coming; it is altogether another thing to be occupying until He DOES come. All around us souls are lost, unprepared to meet God. What am I doing about it? What are YOU doing about it? Souls are precious — too precious in the sight of Jesus — to spend eternity in hell: *"For what is a man profited, if he shall gain the whole world, and lose his own soul? Or what shall a man give in exchange for his soul?"* (Matt. 16:26).

God so loved sinners that He gave the best heaven had, His only begotten Son, that we might be saved. *Jesus* so loved sinners that He bore our sins in His own body on the cross. *The Holy Spirit* so loves sinners that He is in the world to convict, convince, and draw them to the Father.

But WE are the branches, WE must bear the fruit, WE have the glorious opportunity of pointing men to the Lord Jesus Christ for salvation. We need to seek them out, witness to them, tell them about His love and the good news that Jesus saves.

"In such an hour as ye think not, the Son of man cometh!"